Free the Music Business:
Tips and Tales from an Indie Music Nerd

Written by Adam Cruz
Edited by Amanda Frontany
Book cover design by Jose Gonzalez

Distributed by The Cruz Music Group, a division of
Mixtape Sessions Music, LLC.

ISBN 978-1-7328575-0-6 (trade paperback)
ISBN 978-1-7328575-1-3 (e-book)
ISBN 978-1-7328575-2-0 (audiobook)

First Edition: December 21, 2018

Dedicated, with love, to creatives all over the world.

FOREWORD

"Welcome to another edition of the Freedom Radio Hour. I'm your host Adam Cruz and I'm sitting next to my fantastic partner, Eddie Nicholas. We give you music business news and trends from around the globe."

These are the opening lines for our weekly syndicated radio program, the *Freedom Radio Hour*, co-hosted by Adam Cruz and myself. Since 2014, Adam and I have been on a mission to share our insights and thoughts on all things music-business related. Adam brings a wealth of knowledge to our radio show-- knowledge that he has cultivated as a label owner, music distributor, recording artist, studio engineer, and technology specialist. He has a natural talent for taking the often complicated details of music business and communicating them clearly and transparently to music lovers and consumers around the world. It is Adam's belief that music needs to be understood and respected not only as a creative art form, but also as a product with a value. In *Free the Music Business: Tips and Tales from an Indie Music Nerd,* Adam Cruz takes us on a journey to understand how music consumption has changed since the days of the record store to the here and now of online streaming and most importantly, how all parties have been effected. I encourage you to let Adam take you on this journey. If you love music, you need to read this book. It is with great pride that I introduce you to my brother and author Adam Cruz, and his very important and timely book, *Free the Music Business: Tips and Tales from an Indie Music Nerd.*

— Eddie Nicholas, October 2018

ACKNOWLEDGEMENTS

This book would not have been possible without the love, support and encouragement from my wonderful family and friends. Thank you especially to my amazing sister Flora and all of the talented artists at Mixtape Sessions, my dear friend and Freedom Radio Hour co-host Eddie Nicholas, Tim Lawrence, Angelo Ellerbee, Kevin Hedge, Louie Vega, Kenny Dope, Lyn Woods, Andy Luna, Alex Jost, Illya Odessa, Joe Chan, Taha Elroubi and our Capital Radio 91.6FM family in Sudan, Duce Martinez, Gladys Heredia and our D. Wild Music Radio family, Josh Milan, Gloria Milan and our Honeycomb Music family, all of the superb labels distributed by The Cruz Music Group, my love Sarah, our beautiful children: Seyoni, Tamirah and AJ, my loving mom, my gifted niece Victoria, my inspiring cousin Frankala, my encouraging Esther Friedman, Sam Friedman, Rose Ferguson, Robert Friedman, Stephanie Cook and our extended families.

I'd like to especially thank the multi-talented Jose Gonzalez for a fantastic book cover design and of course, thank you to my prima, Amanda Frontany, who made a scary endeavor smooth and sweet with her guidance, input, suggestions and friendship.

You all mean the world to me.

If I've forgotten you, please charge it to my head and not my heart, but know that I appreciate you.

Thank you especially to Music. You are a healer to us all.

"If you feel safe in the area you're working in,
you're not working in the right area.
Always go a little further into the water
than you feel you're capable of being in.
Go a little bit out of your depth.
And when you don't feel that your feet
are quite touching the bottom,
you're just about in the right place
to do something exciting."

— David Bowie

TABLE OF CONTENTS

Chapter 1: New York to New Jersey and Back

New York City seemed to have a burst of warm days after a brutal winter. The spring of 2004 seems like a dream when I think about it now. Much like today, I had a lot of work to do. It was my first day as the A&R and Production Director of this incredibly famous disco label, but I didn't feel nervous or uncomfortable. I suppose I ignored the significance of what was happening in my life much like I ignored the incredibly gorgeous weather on that spring day in Chelsea. Back then, I was doing the daily commuters' *hustle dance* as I called it. I traveled with the masses from train to train commuting from the suburbs of New Jersey to the "center of the universe" – New York City – each of us with our respective master plans in mind. I had it down to a science. I knew which part of the train platform to stand by so that when the doors opened, I had the best chance of finding a seat and positioning myself at the best exit door once I got to my first transfer point — Hoboken. From there, it was just a few stops on the PATH train to 14th Street, NYC. I had been doing the *hustle dance* for months, deepening the work relationships I was developing at West End Records. My birthplace was only a train ride uptown, but it felt like a world away.

Even though I was born uptown at Mount Sinai Hospital, I always lived in New Jersey. As I prepared to write this book, I learned from my mom that she and my late father met in church. Back then, there were seven churches that would come together at various times. My mom's church was based in the Bronx and my dad's was based in Paterson, New Jersey. This is how we ended up growing up in Paterson and living there for over a decade. From what I've been told, as a young man, my dad played some guitar in church and sang beautifully. He once even wrote lyrics and created a hymn using the melody of The Beatles' "Yesterday" and would sing it in church. At 13, my mom remembers writing poetry and being asked to recite a poem she wrote about spiritual life, sin and salvation during the service. Each seemed to have their moments to creatively express themselves, but neither sought to sing and record their own music or publish their own poetry professionally. I, however, had my own ideas.

My cousin is eight years older than I am and was a fantastic DJ in the Bronx. I marveled at him and his friends and how they used certain sections of songs as opportunities to mix into an entirely different song. Back then, it was all about Freestyle music or as some called it, 'Latin Hip Hop.' I never did understand the latter term and no one I knew ever referred to the latest Corina, Safire or Fascination record as 'Latin Hip Hop.' My cousin Frank (*DJ Frankala,* as he was called back then) used to record himself mixing from one song to another, creating a seamless blend. He recorded 60 and 90 minute Maxell or TDK cassette tapes, and he and his friends, Louie Love and Freddy-O, used to blast the latest music on these mix tapes in my Titi Carmen's Fordham Road walk-up apartment. Frank was one of four siblings and no one ever seemed to mind the loud music coming from the stereo. Years later, he would eventually gift me his DJ equipment and record collection, which literally kick-started a lifelong passion to DJ. Freddy-O and Louie Love also gifted me most of their records. I'm still humbled when I think about that.

My mom, my sister Flora and I would regularly visit our family in the Bronx. At that time, most of my family lived in various sections of the Bronx. In fact, we were the only side of the family who lived in Jersey. While I come from a pretty large family (my mom is one of nine children), we were particularly close with Titi Carmen and her kids. I have so many fond memories of hanging with them, but some of these memories are a little fuzzy. You see, my mom was diagnosed with ovarian cancer in the early 80s. She arranged for my sister and me to live with Titi Carmen for a period of time while she underwent a full hysterectomy which led to menopause almost immediately thereafter. I remember spending a lot of time with them, going to school with my cousins and learning how to snap my fingers in front of Ms. Peter's class. I needed to learn that particular skill rather quickly since I was jammin' to some incredible music courtesy of the radio and *DJ Frankala* and I needed an outlet. Finger snapping was it!

At age three, my mom and dad divorced, and when I was seven, my dad, a military man, was in a terrible accident while serving his one-weekend-a-month duty. As best as I can remember, he and two others were in a military jeep and they stopped in a parking lot to have lunch. The driver was drinking and when they got back on the road, the driver headed off either against traffic or didn't see an oncoming tractor trailer. They collided and my dad was the only one severely injured. He spent the better part of a year in a coma and my sister and I were allowed very rare moments to see him. At one point, he was in a hospital in Utica, New York, and later at another facility that didn't allow children much visitation. He suffered severe head trauma and was taken off life support as the winter of 1984 approached. He was given a military-style funeral and I remember hearing the bugle call of "Taps" being played by live trumpeters followed by ceremonial gunshots. For years, I made up that I tried to jump in the casket. I think my eight-year-old mind raced to try to come to grips with goodbye as that casket was lowered into the ground. These moments in my life also added to the closeness I felt with Titi Carmen's family and the escape that the music gave me at an early age. Where other memories of my childhood remain foggy, the music memories always seem crisp and clear. During this time, I realized that music gave off certain therapeutic qualities. It also gave way to theater and drama. Hip Hop offered the possibility of putting your ego on full display. Back then, Hip Hop was in its early days and emcees spent time bragging and boasting about their rapping abilities and their cleverness. In retrospect, the escapism of it all was the most appealing. Who could blame me? In music, I heard characters, stories and messages. It was as if someone out there had been watching my life and could sing or rap about what I was feeling. Music was a great way to deal with the immense pain of having lost my dad in this long, drawn out and brutal way. I needed therapy, but didn't seek counseling. I was a kid with no real choices and it just wasn't a thing to do back then. I used music. I remembered the lyrics of the songs I loved and even the songs I hated. Don't you hate it when you sometimes remember the songs you hate the most? I'd sing them along as each played on the radio and I loved pretending to be the character in the story being sung or the track being rapped to. It was a safe and non-judgmental utopia for me.

In his book *The Future of Music: Manifesto for a Digital Music Revolution*, writer David Kusek describes a multimedia utopia. In it, you wake up to sounds of music from a playlist you set for mornings. All of the rooms in your home, from the bedroom to the bathroom to the kitchen, are all equipped with a way to listen to music, watch a film, or read a book. Forget the *iWhatever*. You don't need any of that in this scenario. The device is you and you are the device. Initially, I was deeply fascinated and slightly jealous. I mean, with a futuristic media system throughout every room, Kusek described an idyllic environment from which to consume music at every instance and in every inch of your home. His descriptions reminded me of *The Minority Report*, a movie that Tom Cruise starred in. In the title role, Cruise was one of the detectives in a "pre-crimes unit" — a futuristic crime-fighting police station that worked to stop crimes before they were committed. Imagine, for a moment, the implications of a society run in that way. I watched in amazement as Cruise's character was able to use his fingers to form a box shape which then manifested itself into a screen in midair. As part of this pre-crimes unit, he was charged with looking for the possibility of crimes. I was instantly fascinated not just by that kind of movie plot, but by the idea of instantly accessing a holographic screen by making invisible box shapes with your fingers. After reading Kusek's book, I imagined being able to use my hands to form a screen in midair. From there, I not only could listen to music, but create it, mix it, master it, and release it as well.

Kusek really inspired me. He argued that artists and content creators alike ought to consider music as a public utility model. I'll tell you more about all of that later, but it was Kusek that led me to think not just about music as a public utility model, but also about the hyper holographic experience for consuming media. It reminded me that we can think bigger and be larger than even our biggest dreams. As a society, we've made such advancements in music technology over the years. We've gone from vinyl, this large tangible product, to streaming, an invisible product. We've gone from the large Victrola to a hand-held device that fits in our pocket. Just like the dramatic evolution of music products and devices, the same applies to how artists get paid (or don't) in this evolution. Music royalties, a contentious topic for any working artist, became more elusive in the age of digital music. I suppose I'm jumping ahead a bit, but it's always been my belief that much of this elusiveness dissipates once the artists move closer to a transparent payment system. Open source, transparency and knowledge sharing are key elements. Kusek imagined translucent devices with instant access to media, but it always bothered me that no one had thought of something similar to make it easier to see how money flowed between artists, music publishers and record labels. It further bothered me that, with all of this imagined innovation, we hadn't yet imagined a system for extracting money that creatives earn from music. David Kusek published The *Future of Music: Manifesto for a Digital Music Revolution* in 2005 and over a dozen years later, we're still waiting for a revolution around systems for royalty administration and payments.[1]

So what would I envision? In short, I envision a simple and transparent system between artists that negates the effects of manual interplay. For the most part, artists tend to get signed to major and minor deals based on the fundamental premise that one entity gets the money.

---

[1] Kusek, D. (2005). *The Future of Music: Manifesto for a Digital Music Revolution*. Boston: Berklee Press.

The artist then agrees to let that entity determine and issue a royalty statement, and subsequently distribute earned royalties to the artist. The entity can be a record label, a music publisher or even another independent artist. This structure mandates that one receives the funds and then shares the funds to the other. The big elephant in the room we're not discussing is the 'honor system' that artists are left to enact in this arrangement. I can spend the rest of this book detailing the atrocities that have occurred between artists, their families and the record labels that owed them royalties, but I think the main point would be overstated. What artists need the most is a simple way to navigate the system that removes the need to enact an honor system. Imagine for the rest of this book that you're an artist or content creator. Your undying wish is to be able to create and live off of your creations for the rest of your life. You've tried before and perhaps trusted someone who took your share of the proceeds or fiscally misguided you in some way. In other instances, you might have gotten little return or felt dismayed to continue. What was the biggest hurdle? Was it the lack of funds? Was it the lack of royalty reporting? Was it the lack of steady communication from the other entity?

If I were interested in working on a song with a particular artist (in this utopian ideal), there would be a system to send communication that formally requests a collaboration. All parties would already be registered and have accounts set up where necessary. As an artist, you can choose to work within the existing banking system or can elect to work within a bitcoin-related system. In simple terms, bitcoin technology makes it possible to issue payments without manual interplay.

As an artist, I don't have to trust you to send me my 50% that we agreed upon as payment for our collaborative song. With a transparent system, I can see all of the money earned on our song without asking or needing to wait for payment. Each time someone purchases or streams our song, we each instantly receive notification that we've received new income, where it came from, when we received funds and more. Every royalty earned would be instantly reported and paid out to all involved. In a bitcoin-related system, banks cannot freeze, allow garnishing or engage in fractional reserve banking, the practice whereby a bank accepts deposits, makes loans or investments, and holds reserves that are a fraction of its deposit liabilities.[2]

Beyond these issues, it is also important to recognize that half the world does not even have a bank account. In a 2012 *Bloomberg Technology* article, author Karen Weise explains that "in the U.S., bank accounts are nearly ubiquitous, with almost 90 percent of adults having formal accounts. But in poor countries, only a quarter of people report having had accounts. All told, more than 2.5 billion adults around the world—about half—are unbanked, according to a new World Bank data project funded by the Bill & Melinda Gates Foundation and based on Gallup polling in 148 countries."[3] In 2016, the World Economic Forum published an article, reporting that over 2 billion people worldwide were unbanked.

---

[2] Money, S. (2015, November 24). Fractional-Reserve Banking is Pure Fraud, Part I. Web: http://www.zerohedge.com/news/2015-11-23/fractional-reserve-banking-pure-fraud-part-i

[3] Weise, K. (2012, April 25). Why Half the World Doesn't Have Bank Accounts. Bloomberg Technology. Web: https://www.bloomberg.com/news/articles/2012-04-25/why-half-the-world-doesnt-have-bank-accounts

The article explains:

> [T]he World Bank (WB) has set an ambitious goal of securing universal access to formal financial services by 2020. Although 700 million people have signed up for a bank account since 2011, about two billion worldwide remain unbanked. As the WB seeks to expand worldwide financial inclusion, it should look to Sub-Saharan Africa (SSA) for inspiration. In the developing world as a whole, 54% of adults have an account – up 13 percentage points since 2011, according to the Global Findex database. The vast majority of that growth came from people opening accounts at banks or other financial institutions. Sub-Saharan Africa is the only developing region to defy this trend. In part, by harnessing mobile money technology, through mobile money service accounts and the increase in bank agents that use mobile phones to reach rural clients, SSA drove up account ownership by a third – to 34%. Overall, 12% of adults in the region have a mobile money account, which is four times the developing world average.[4]

Banking is not only a global endeavor, but it's being pushed as aspirational. While I agree that we need good mechanisms to allow people to easily exchange money and that a growing amount of transactions are occurring via a mobile device, I don't believe that we should be co-signing for a global push towards regulated bank accounts like most of us have in the United States. The money you've

---

[4] Asktrakhan, I. (2016, May 17). 2 billion people worldwide are unbanked – here's how to change this. Web: https://www.weforum.org/agenda/2016/05/2-billion-people-worldwide-are-unbanked-heres-how-to-change-this

been using all your life is backed by a government of some sort, and it exists in a tangible way. Bitcoin, for example, is neither tangible nor backed by anyone, but it's still worth a great deal to some people. This digital currency began circulating on the Internet in 2009 with each Bitcoin worth just a tiny bit of "real" money, but right now a single Bitcoin is worth more than $2,000. Bitcoin is fascinating from a technological standpoint, but it's also fueling online crime and violence because of the anonymity it offers.

Here's how Bitcoin works and why you should care.

What is Bitcoin?

Bitcoin is what's known as cryptocurrency, a digital asset that exists only as data. You probably have money in the bank that is digital, but those digits equal physical currency. Not so with Bitcoin. Bitcoin also has no centralized regulation nor innate legal framework. As such, the value of Bitcoin is dictated entirely by the market, and the market is hot right now. Bitcoin is stored in a digital wallet, which you can save locally on a hard drive or phone, or online with any number of Bitcoin exchanges. Saving your Bitcoins locally is like keeping all your money under the mattress. If something happens to the digital wallet, all your money is toast. Sending and receiving money is handled by pointing your Bitcoin client or web exchange toward a Bitcoin address, which every wallet has. A few minutes later, the Bitcoin will leave your wallet and show up in another.

Websites that accept Bitcoin are rare, but they are out there. Spending it in real life is considerably trickier, but again, there are a few systems in place to manage it.[5] Beyond cryptocurrency and bitcoin technology, the message is clear that the U.S. and all of us ought to think beyond the status quo or the traditional mechanisms for fiscally connecting fans and artists. We ought to recognize the possibilities that exist for instant remuneration with no manual interplay. When you think about it, we have forms of this already. Bandcamp, CDbaby, TuneCore and many other websites offer digital distribution, real-time reporting, promotional features and more, for a fee. What I'm envisioning goes much deeper than the traditional platform. Oftentimes there is more to it than reporting each download or stream count. It's also about reporting and sending funds to the other parties involved in creating that content. For every dollar earned, artists have to then share a percentage of that dollar with several others. In most digital music scenarios, that dollar is split between you, any co-writers, performers and "processors."

In this context, a processor can be PayPal (an online mechanism for sending and receiving funds), digital music distributors like Bandcamp or TuneCore and others. In my utopia, none would need to exist except content creators and an open source, transparent royalty system. Unlike on other platforms, my idyllic environment would also instantly manage the various types of rights for each artist all in one place. Right now, your rights are generally divided into various categories and are managed by several different organizations, as follows:

---

[5] Whitwam, R. (2017, May 18). Bitcoin Is Bigger Than Ever, And Here's Why That Matters. Forbes. Web: https://tinyurl.com/yb7d2csz

Public Performing Right
The exclusive right of the copyright owner, granted by the U.S. Copyright Law, to authorize the performance or transmission of the work in public.

Public Performance License
Performance rights organizations issue licenses on behalf of the copyright owner or his or her agent granting the right to perform the work in, or transmit the work to, the public.

Reproduction Right
The exclusive right of the copyright owner, granted by the Copyright Act, to authorize the reproduction of a musical work as in a record, cassette or CD.

Mechanical License
Harry Fox Agency, Inc. issues licenses on behalf of the copyright owner or his or her agent, usually to a record company, granting the record company the right to reproduce and distribute a specific composition at an agreed upon fee per unit manufactured and sold.

Synchronization License
Music Publishers issue licenses as copyright owner or his or her agent, usually to a producer, granting the right to synchronize the musical composition in timed relation with audio-visual images on film or videotape.

Digital Performance Right in Sound Recordings
Sound Exchange along with Record Companies license the exclusive rights on behalf of copyright owners in a sound recording under U.S. Copyright Law to authorize many digital transmissions (e.g., Internet streaming).[6]

You see the dilemma? Ok . . . right. I can release my own music using an independent means, but they (co-writers, performers and "processors") will take something to make that possible.

In addition, once the funds are received, there are further splits that need to occur. Who or what handles this? Furthermore, there are a few income streams to consider and manage that go beyond the typical download dollar.

Back on that 2007 spring day in NYC, the furthest thing on my mind was royalty administration, but little did I know that *royalties* were going to be the topic of conversation dozens of times more in the coming years.

---

[6] BMI (2017). Types of Copyright. Web:
https://www.bmi.com/licensing/entry/types_of_copyrights

Chapter 2: West End and the Wild Wild West

New York City was a hotbed of inspiration in 2004, but I'm sure almost everyone has a year that inspired them the most. For me, it happened because of New York City. It's that kind of place. It dawned on me that I was now working for a highly respected record label (with a proud history in NYC) and my perspective of the indie music community had changed. It was as if a 'tipping point' was occurring in my life and I felt strongly about honoring it. In his book *The Tipping Point: How Little Things Can Make a Big Difference*, author Malcolm Gladwell defines the 'tipping point' as "the moment of critical mass, the threshold, the boiling point." Gladwell argues that "ideas and products and messages and behaviors spread like viruses do."[7] Because West End has such an illustrious past and the opinions about its future were aggressive, we operated as three labels in one: West End Classics, West End Records and West End Tracks. We worked to reissue all of the many disco classics that made the label famous, then signed and released new vocal acts. As to not ignore the burgeoning electronic dance music (EDM) market, we also signed and released non-vocal tracks. Initially, our audience was made up of nostalgics, vinyl collectors and *house heads* — a term coined for lovers of a style of dance music called *house music*. Its derivative? Disco! Enter West End Records.

---

[7] Gladwell, M. (2000). The Tipping Point: How Little Things Can Make a Big Difference. Boston: Little Brown & Company.

West End had experienced a rise and fall, a dormant period, followed by a re-emergence with two predecessors before I even got there. With an almost thirty-year history, I don't know that I quite understood the enormity of the job I had accepted. As A&R and Production Director, I was in charge of juggling an active vinyl production schedule for over two dozen catalog reissues. It meant being on the phone and writing emails for a good chunk of the day. There were credits to collect, vinyl labels to print up, mastering jobs to pick up, test pressings to approve, 12" jackets with cut out holes to manufacture, and distributors to follow up with. All of this had to be well-timed and orchestrated. All the while, artists were receiving advance amounts that diminished over time. On the surface, you'd think that all was fiscally vibrant, but I learned that all of the components to release a record cost money upfront and while you wait for distributors to pay on the vinyl you ship them, you can quickly go bankrupt if you're not careful. It all felt like a bit of a balancing act or a dance that could easily fall flat if a fiscal miscalculation was made. On top of all this, artists began to call to ask for their royalty statements. For whatever reason, there wasn't a royalty administration system in place for these new signings and I knew we couldn't simply tally up vinyl sales against expenses and advances. There was way more to it and it was more complicated than that. Enter the cost analysis.

I created a spreadsheet that calculated expenses against earnings, which included details about a new revenue stream — digital download sales. From our website, you could buy and download most of the West End catalog. All around me, the culture felt as though it was against the digital download because it effected vinyl sales.

Diehard fans were against it because they were pro-analog and pro-vinyl. Distributors were against it because it diminished their bottom line. So, we had to create a policy where we released material on vinyl first and then later, digitally. I didn't realize it, but our technique of staggering the releases is a strategy called *windowing*. It seemed to both work and not work all at the same time. It worked because it provided this additional revenue stream for West End and later, would propel us to consider our first 'iTunes' like store with other labels. As an industry, we had already succumbed to the business model of the iTunes music store which had launched in April 2003. Miles away and a year earlier in Cupertino, California, Steve Jobs and leaders of Apple, a huge computer company, had invited two of the biggest labels, Warner Music and Universal, to discuss Jobs' vision for an online music download store. Reports during this time indicate that the labels were most concerned with addressing dwindling album sales which they blamed on illegal piracy sites like Napster and MP3.com. All the while, technology was rapidly changing how we consume music and the music industry had no real grasp of what lie ahead. As always it seemed as though the recording industry response to piracy was to continue fighting its sources while letting technology companies dictate how their music was going to be consumed and valued online. The industry couldn't possibly keep up with the burgeoning demands of digital music whether legal or illegal. One can't ignore that Steve Jobs and Apple must have known this and used it to their advantage. Why wouldn't they? They were already working on the next generation of the iPod, their mobile device. It synced the media you were buying in the iTunes store to something you could take on the go.

This is why Apple needed the labels on board, but for these labels to sign, there were hurdles. Initially, the labels rejected downloadable music arguing that it would spell the death of the album. In a digital music world, Apple knew it would be best to give the customer the opportunity to download each track separately from and in addition to the full album. In exchange for enabling this feature, Warner Music and Universal wanted two main issues addressed: the number of CD burns allowed and the number of computers authorized to access the same library's contents. This is the beginning of DRM or *digital rights management*. After all, the iTunes music store acted as retail store, digital music library organizer, CD burning dashboard, and syncing portal for the iPod. The third generation of the iPod was released on April 28, 2003, the day of the store's launch. The music industry didn't know what hit it. After Apple agreed to restrict the number of computers authorized to access that library to three and the number of times a playlist can be burned onto a CD to seven, Warner Music and Universal signed. EMI, BMG and Sony soon followed. It didn't seem to be the big deal that, in retrospect, we know it turned out to be at the time. Apple was offering the music through their store, which was available only to MAC users at the time.[8] With this deal predating the explosion of the smartphone that was to come, there was certainly no way the music business could predict nor keep up. Think about it. Major record labels were signing a deal to make their music available as digital downloads. In this current age of streaming music, this seems so basic and old, but there certainly can't be a step two without a step one.

---

[8] Chen, B. (2010, April 28). April 28, 2003: Apple Opens iTunes Store. Wired. Web: https://goo.gl/DkVudQ

Unfortunately, there isn't nearly enough information about another big item that dramatically changed the way we value music. The iTunes store offered the music at 99¢ per track . . . let that sink in for a moment. Each song that an artist created, spent time recording and perfecting was valued at less than a dollar. Who decided that? Steve Jobs. Evidently, Jobs favored this price because of its simplicity for consumers.[9] So a tech person dictated the price for songs made by artists. Not the artists. In all fairness, we can't ignore what was happening to music before the Apple deal. The RIAA (the Recording Industry Association of America) had spent considerable time and resources fighting peer-to-peer file sharing services like Napster, but with questionable results. With a quick download and installation of Napter's software, you could access, download and share folders containing music files from other users. This was the beginning of the digital music "Wild Wild West." Napster was founded by Shawn Fanning, John Fanning and Sean Parker and operated (in its original incarnation) between June 1999 and July 2001. Once Napster and other similar sites like MP3.com were forced to shut down, it sent a clear signal. While the RIAA was willing to spend money, time and resources to fight digital music piracy and force Napster to shut down, it was winning the battle while losing the war. In their book *Playing for Change: Music and Musicians in the Service of Social Movements,* authors Richard Flacks and Rob Rosenthal so eloquently explain the industry response to piracy.

---

[9] Chaffin, J., Allison, K. (2006, May 1). Apple sets tune for pricing of song downloads. Financial Times. Web: https://goo.gl/Fz8K4n

In it, they argue that:

> the industry responded with a three-pronged strategy:
> (1) a public relations campaign around the theme of
> downloading as theft; (2) a technological approach
> that included both installing digital rights
> management systems (DRMs) on CDs to prevent
> duplication and 'pollution' attacks that sent bugs and
> corrupted files into P2P [peer-to-peer] networks; and
> (3) a legal strategy of suing P2P sites like Napster, as
> well as individual downloaders, for copyright
> infringement.[10]

It always fascinated and saddened me that the RIAA spent
so much time on their public relations campaign around the
theme of downloading as theft. Remember back in 2003,
when the RIAA, in an effort to fight piracy, began suing
private citizens, including teenagers? From a Fox News
report, here's that old story:

> Brianna LaHara said she was frightened to learn she
> was among the hundreds of people sued yesterday by
> giant music companies in federal courts around the
> country. "I got really scared. My stomach is all
> turning," Brianna said last night at the city Housing
> Authority apartment where she lives with her mom
> and her 9-year-old brother.
>
> "I thought it was OK to download music because my
> mom paid a service fee for it. Out of all people, why
> did they pick me?"

---

[10] Rosenthal, R., Flacks, R. (2016). Playing for Change: Music and
Musicians in the Service of Social Movements. New York: Routledge.

The Recording Industry Association of America — a music-industry lobbying group behind the lawsuits — couldn't answer that question. "We are taking each individual on a case-by-case basis," said RIAA spokeswoman Amy Weiss.

Asked if the association knew Brianna was 12 when it decided to sue her, Weiss answered, "We don't have any personal information on any of the individuals." Brianna's mom, Sylvia Torres, said the lawsuit was a total shock. "My daughter was on the verge of tears when she found out about this," Torres said. The family signed up for the Kazaa (search) music-swapping service three months ago, and paid a $29.99 service charge.

Usually, they listen to songs without recording them. "There's a lot of music there, but we just listen to it and let it go," Torres said. When reporters visited the apartment last night, Brianna — who her mom says is an honors student — was helping her brother with his homework. Brianna was among 261 people sued for copying thousands of songs via a popular Internet file-sharing software — and thousands more suits could be on the way. "Nobody likes playing the heavy and having to resort to litigation," said Cary Sherman, the RIAA's president. "But when your product is being regularly stolen, there comes a time when you have to take appropriate action."

At the same time, the RIAA offered amnesty to file-swappers who come forward and agree to stop illegally downloading music over the Internet. People who already have been sued are not eligible for amnesty. Brianna and the others sued yesterday under federal copyright law could face penalties of up to $150,000 per song, but the RIAA has already settled some cases for as little as $3,000. "It's not like we were doing anything illegal," said Torres. "This is a 12-year-old girl, for crying out loud."[11]

Media sharing wasn't going anywhere though. We were already enjoying software apps like AOL Instant Messenger where chatting and file sharing were happening regularly. I'm talking back when apps were called *applications* and instant messaging was changing electronic mail. The music business was slow to react and respond then and is slow to react and respond today. In April 2007, Apple announced that their 100 millionth iPod had been sold.[12] Did these major labels negotiate for a share of the income earned from the sales of iPods? After all, Steve Jobs thought these labels were so essential to the success of the iPod. Did these major labels own shares in Apple?

By late spring of 2006 when labels re-negotiated their initial deal with Apple, the most significant fight seemed to be towards variable pricing, a tiered pricing model that would allow Apple to charge more for new material from top artists.

---

[11] Staff Writer. (2003, September 9). 12-Year-Old Sued for Music Downloading. Fox News. Web: https://goo.gl/3nEDiH

[12] Press Release. (2007, April 9). 100 Million iPods Sold. Apple. Web: https://goo.gl/XTy5np

In the over ten years since this re-negotiation, the price per download has never gone higher than $1.29 per song. Thirty cents. By the time Apple experienced its one millionth iPod sale, the digital download was king. It was the main mode of music consumption for many music lovers. Vinyl and CDs were heavy, took up space and didn't allow you to buy just one song. Labels were right to fear the demise of the album once digital downloads became available on a per-track basis. Albums have long since fallen out of favor. Today, the playlist is the album. Listeners didn't want to buy just one song on an album. They also wanted to make their own albums in the form of playlists. Forget one artist. Now, users could choose an unlimited amount of artists and songs thereby creating their own listening experience. On the upside, it was very convenient. You could store hundreds of songs on an iPod and listen on the go. On the downside, no longer was there value placed on owning music, reading liner notes nor fully appreciating an album's artwork, for example.

While Apple enjoyed billions in profits by April 2007, music consumption was rapidly changing all around them. A website for video content called *YouTube* launched in February 2005 and was growing in popularity faster than expected. Even Apple wasn't fully prepared for what was going to occur in the fall of 2008 when a small streaming music company called *Spotify* launched. Spotify operated under a *freemium* model (basic services are free, while additional features are offered via paid subscriptions). Spotify makes its revenues by selling premium streaming subscriptions to users and advertising to third parties. This turned the digital download model upside down. Who cares about owning an album or a CD? Who cares about owning a digital download on your computer?

You don't need to own any music if you can access it anytime you want. To boot, it was free. Forget 99¢ or $1.29. To pay for a subscription to Spotify, it is as low as $9.99 a month for unlimited access to their entire catalog of songs. The question for any artist on the service then became: *how can I compete with free*? How can an artist help promote, market and encourage fans to buy music when listeners can access it for free? *Freemium* became a hot button issue for artists like Taylor Swift who argued that Spotify made millions from streaming hit songs without fair compensation. For each listen, an artist earns a fraction of a penny.

Not left unscathed, YouTube was also under fire. While it started as a video content site, it was user-generated. This meant that users could upload all kinds of content in different ways. In addition, YouTube users regularly uploaded music, music videos and fan-made content. Problems with streaming payouts ensued. For example, author Todd Frankel (in a recent *Washington Post* article) noted that "musicians from Arcade Fire to Garth Brooks to Pharrell Williams say they earn significantly less when their songs are played on YouTube than on a site such as Spotify — even though many listeners use these services in the same way. Both YouTube and Spotify allow users to search for music and find song recommendations. On YouTube, users can find music alongside cat videos and toy reviews in what is generally a free-for-all of content, while people go to Spotify and the like for a more refined experience. Some audiophiles argue the sound quality of music streaming sites is superior.

YouTube pays an estimated $1 per 1,000 plays on average, while Spotify and Apple music pay a rate closer to $7. Irving Azoff, the legendary manager for acts such as the Eagles and Christina Aguilera, said he has one artist — whom he declined to name — who gets 33 percent of her online streams from YouTube, but only 10 percent of her streaming revenue. Smaller acts see it too. Zoe Keating, an instrumental cello player, showed *The Washington Post* a statement from YouTube showing that she earned $261 from 1.42 million views on YouTube. In comparison, she earned $940 from 230,000 streams on Spotify. Keating told the *Post,* "YouTube revenue is so negligible that I stopped paying attention to it." YouTube admits that it pays less for songs. But the reason for this disparity is where the two sides split.

The music industry claims that YouTube has avoided paying a fair-market rate by hiding behind broad legal protections. In the United States, that's the 'safe harbor' provision, which essentially says YouTube is not to blame if someone uploads a copy-protected song — unless the copyright holder complains. YouTube says it has the solution: its Content ID system automatically checks for violations by comparing songs detected in new uploads against a database of claimed songs, capturing 99.5 percent of complaints. The company says it averages fewer than 1,500 traditional copyright claims from the music industry a week.[13]

---

[13] Frankel, T. (2017, July 14). Why musicians are so angry at the world's most popular music streaming service. Washington Post. Web: https://goo.gl/UVUjpJ

So, as long as YouTube continues operating its Content ID system, it indemnifies itself from copyright infringement claims. But, the issue isn't just about the safe harbor provision. The artists mentioned in that *Washington Post* piece are also shining a light on another big problem plaguing artists — *value gap*.

In an annual report published in 2016 by the International Federation of the Phonographic Industry (IFPI), services like YouTube draw the world's biggest audience of music fans, but only pay out about 4 percent of total revenue to labels and artists. YouTube is the biggest service of its kind, estimated by technology analysis firm MIDiA Research, to draw 800 million monthly music video viewers. But YouTube and similar services that make money from advertising paid out a small amount of the global revenues that help artists and labels stay in business and create. The amount is so low, a trade group said, that revenue from ad-supported streaming generated less money than vinyl records in some big music markets like the United States.

IFPI represents the interests of the music industry globally. A YouTube spokesperson responded that Google has paid out more than $3 billion to the music industry overall, and said that in recent years, only about 20 percent of people have historically been willing to pay for music. "YouTube is helping artists and labels monetize the remaining 80 percent," its spokesperson said. YouTube also launched a paid tier last year in which members contribute revenue to the music industry. And the music videos that tend to get the most views are the ones from labels.

Consumers are shifting from paying to own music to paying services that stream music and make money from subscriptions or advertising.[14]

While YouTube's value gap problem seems to be a relatively new phenomenon, this isn't the first time the music industry has experienced a value gap. In this context, the precursor to YouTube was Apple. To me, Apple's version of this value gap issue began the moment that major record labels allowed Jobs to fully execute his marketing vision for that 99¢ per track price point. Apple continued earning profits on the sales of their iPods while labels ignored the fact that Apple built their iPod business off the back of the music industry. If the labels weren't going to baulk, why would Apple? Apple could always point to the millions that labels have made from iTunes sales while Apple was off making billions. This again was the first value gap crisis that the music business faced and it failed because it completely ignored it. As a business, we cut ourselves off at the knee to begin with. Ask yourself: when you apply for a job and you get to the part of the interview process where you discuss salary, would you purposely push for a lower salary or a higher one? Once you're locked in, you can only go up but so much within each evaluation period. The same applies in this case.

The labels didn't have enough forethought and knowledge about the benefits of digital music access. They let Jobs have his 99¢ way. Labels could have pushed for a higher price to begin with or again argued for shares in Apple or shares in the sales of the iPod.

---

[14] Solsman, J. (2016, April 12). Study: Streaming Isn't Killing the Music Business — YouTube Is. The Wrap. Web: http://www.thewrap.com/study-streaming-isnt-killing-the-music-business-youtube-is/

This didn't happen. The music industry had an opportunity to learn its mistakes after this issue with Apple, but didn't. Apple's value gap issue (in the form of a 99¢ pricing model) went unaddressed and so today, we have to contend with YouTube's value gap issue.

If we don't learn from the sins of our past, we are doomed to repeat them. Isn't that how the saying goes?

Issues with value gap aren't happening in a bottle though. These issues are connected to and exasperated by an already growing problem with music devaluation. Again: *how do you compete with free?* Amazon, one of the biggest companies in the world, understands the streaming music business well and seems to have taken a cue from Apple's successful iPod playbook. To begin with, Amazon is not new to digital music consumption. While iTunes and Spotify certainly shined, Amazon too launched a digital download site called Amazon MP3 in 2008. They were smart in that they expanded upon their already blossoming product fulfillment business and it made sense that Amazon would engage with music delivery systems like Amazon MP3. Fast forward to 2016 and Amazon launched the Amazon Echo speaker, a hands-free speaker you control with your voice. For buying the speaker, you could also enjoy unlimited music streaming for as low as $5 a month. Later, Amazon released Echo Dot, a smaller version of the Echo speaker (with limited features) as well as Echo Tap and Echo Show. All of these voice-controlled devices each have their own price points and features. So far, Amazon is enjoying a spike in sales of the Echo brand ahead of the previous year.

In the near future, Amazon plans to add cameras to the Echo devices, sending a clear message to Apple that they're in the device-selling business for the long haul.

However, the industry is once again ignoring the re-emergence of the value gap issue it keeps experiencing.

This time, the value gap issue relates to the income being generated from the sales of Amazon Echo speakers, the low price point for streaming music and the over dependence on music to sell a product while only paying out a fraction of a penny-per-stream. It is also worth noting that this fraction of a penny is paid to the labels and music publishers and not necessarily directly paid to the artists that perform on the song.

West End was ever the microcosm, dealing with issues that put us further behind the technological times. We were still arguing about *per download* price points while missing the bigger picture. When iTunes offered music at 99¢ per track, the best solution we could come up with was to increase the per download rate from $1.99 to $2.99 per download. We then *windowed* the digital release. The initial release date, because it's considered the height of interest, was priced at $2.99 per download. After a period of time, the price per download would drop to $1.99. We weren't alone. Soon, another digital download site would emerge with similar intentions crushing our hopes of becoming dance music's answer to iTunes.

As all of this was happening, I prepared to send the next round of royalty statements to our artists and pay them.

Chapter 3: Disco in the Digital Age

In 2001, the Global Music Report estimated that the music industry generated revenue of $23.6 billion. The following year, Napster launched its stable release and the industry lost 40% of its revenue in the succeeding 15 years-- its worst decline of all time. Fast forward to 2016 and the digital streaming revenues account for over 50% of the $15.7 billion total generated revenue. This is also the first time, since Napster, that there have been two years of revenue growth.[15] Back in 2001, there were glimpses of what the future of music would be like. Of course, it's hard to predict the details, but the details are usually the most important parts. Because digital downloads were considered the predominant format for listening to music, it came as no surprise that the market responded. Several digital download sites emerged and all of them seemed to offer the same download experience — click. buy. download. The law of supply and demand was keenly at work in this online digital space. As music lovers, we went from vinyl, cassette and CDs as the main sales drivers, to this invisible digital product, priced at a fraction of what we used to pay. The music being sold at a physical retail store was comparatively higher in price than at a digital download store on the web. Vinyl records cost anywhere from $4.99-$7.99. CDs cost upward of $12.99-15.99. Without realizing it, we were forced to confront this notion of access vs. ownership.

---

[15] Watling, T. (2017, June 30). From sales to streaming. Palatinate. Web: https://goo.gl/LNhtEi

We had been treating music as a tangible good for so long that it's no wonder we became so strongly attached to the MP3 — a computer file essentially. Who could blame us? It was our last hope of ownership. The MP3 became the new CD and the digital download its new majesty. By 2001 and the years that soon followed, digital download retail stores popped up everywhere and rapidly expanded with the same business model at hand. They all vied for your 99¢ or similar. If we as a music industry bothered to notice, we would've realized then that we had become completely dependent on a separate industry altogether (technology) to drive our own music business. We mistakenly treated digital download stores just like the old mom and pop stores of yesteryear. This to me is one of three glaring mistakes that West End and the wider music business made as this digital format was experiencing its own coming-of-age. The fact was that digital download stores weren't at all like the old physical retail stores even though they were dressed in the same way. Yes, with the iTunes store you could browse titles, explore featured artists' profiles, search and buy. This is nearly identical to the physical store experience. On the other hand, the digital download music experience left a lot to be desired. No longer could you hold your music products in your hands before buying them. No longer could you congregate all together and nod your head to the music being heard at a store. No longer could you discover something new while intending to search for something else. No longer could you be drawn in by a wall of cool artwork on album covers. At the digital download store, you are all alone thumbing through tiny thumbnail images for your prospective purchase.

But the funny thing is . . . no one really put up a fuss about this hugely impactful cultural shift. There wasn't a formal response nor a public outcry. In fact, we championed for more convenience and mobility. Apple listened and put it all together for us. Your phone was your music library and your media center. Your phone was your VCR, laserdisc player, 8 track player, turntable, cassette deck, and radio station all in one. Your phone was your online and offline storage and your address book. Our old fashion multimedia sources were now compacted into this new phenomenon called a *smartphone*. In the spring of 2003, Apple launched their iTunes music store thanks in large part to major record labels, but music was just a small part. At a Macworld convention in January 2007, Jobs announced that Apple's first iPhone would be released and on June 29th of that year, the first was offered. Now synced to the iTunes music store, Apple's first iPhone acted as music, TV show, film, book, and communications center. It's worth noting that less than ten years after that announcement, Apple's "valuation reached $1 trillion, close to 70 times the size of the global music industry's worth. For Apple, music practically is the lighter sold at the convenience-store register."[16]

Niche market music took a different stance in terms of the 99¢ argument. In house music, for example, much of our buying audience is made up of DJs and those who aspire to have a DJ's music collection. Enter Traxsource.com.

I mentioned earlier that West End once aspired to become its own kind of iTunes store. The vision was to make the

[16] Parker, C. (2015, September 16). Streaming's Poised to Save the Music Business. Now Apple's Ready to Take Over. Phoenix New Times. Web: https://goo.gl/m91kfK

West End website a one-stop shop for a certain brand of niche market music that we validated or co-signed. Because of West End's proud history, we were hoping to capitalize on its respected brand to then help propel the label to become the first online store of its kind. To us, iTunes was fast becoming a bastion of quickly produced music that lacked the qualities that made West End synonymous with class and distinction. We thought that we could align our brand with other brands online. However by October 2004, a new digital download site emerged that trounced any of our efforts. Traxsource.com launched in the fall of that year by co-founders Marc Pomeroy and Brian Tappert, and quickly established itself as the main source for the style of dance music that West End was most aligned with and was hoping to monetize from. Today, Traxsource.com distributes music from over 20,000 labels and 250,000 artists. At first, we tried launching our own online store, signing over half a dozen labels to digital distribution deals. Given our ongoing vinyl production efforts, some of these digital partnerships used us as leverage to then venture into vinyl distribution. In short: it didn't work. Why? Whenever vinyl distributors heard previews of our associates' latest releases, it didn't quite capture the magic of the sound of West End. In my opinion, anyone we put forward was compared to West End and subsequently failed in this comparison. The other issue was the way in which we were operating West End Records itself. Because we compartmentalized the releases using the names West End Classics, West End Records, West End Blue and West End Tracks, I think it confused our loyal audience. Furthermore, there's always a shelf life in terms of an old record label catering to its nostalgic audience. You can only remix the classics so many times or re-package a hit single in a new way so many times.

When we tried, nothing worked better than the original. It taught me a valuable lesson about being original. Part of anyone's story of success includes that element of originality. Running a record label is no different in this regard.

During digital music's coming-of-age, there was a perfect storm of circumstances that changed everything. Until digital music production really took off and you aspired to produce music, you needed to spend thousands of dollars in studio time, musician fees, mixing costs, and much more. You needed a lot of advanced training and a lot of know how. It all seemed to cost more than most of us could afford. But in the digital age, music production occurs with the purchase of a synthesizer, drum sampler and computer. Even today, you can get all of those things in one computer. It's a lot more affordable to make a record these days as compared to how much it used to cost. Today, you can even make and record music directly from your phone. These simple facts challenge our beliefs about what it takes to deliver quality music to the world. For instance, Grammy-nominated musician Steve Lacy recorded the entirety of his six-track EP using just his iPhone. The 19-year old, best known as the guitarist and vocalist for band The Internet, recorded *Steve Lacy's Demo* using his handset while he was touring the world and during studio sessions. While he used music software Ableton to program some of the album's drum beats, the bass, guitar and his vocals were recorded using GarageBand, Apple's own music app. However, Steve Lacy is by no means the first musician to take advantage of Apple's music software capabilities. Pop star Rihanna's 2007 smash hit record "Umbrella" famously uses a standard GarageBand drum loop, and Fall Out Boy, Oasis and Kate Nash have all recorded songs using similar loops and methods.[17] So, creativity can happen at any time and can occur anywhere, and a hit song can cost thousands to make or can cost very little. In years prior, labels would spend millions on making a record. Guns N' Roses is a clear example of this. In the 2005 *New York Times* article "The Most Expensive Album Never Made," a "recording expert" who was present for some of the recording of *Chinese Democracy* said that:

> Guns N' Roses front man Axl Rose wanted to make "the best record that had ever been made. It's an impossible task. You could go on infinitely, which is what they've done." Signed to Geffen Records, label head David Geffen's documents claimed that over $13 million was spent in production costs; the label actually saved money after promising Rose $1 million if he delivered *Chinese Democracy* at a certain time, a deadline Rose would miss by almost 10 years. The $13 million price tag accumulated from the monthly payrolls. Each band member received $11,000, guitar technicians $6000, the chief engineer $14,000, the recording software engineer $25,000. Rental of the studio itself cost $50,000 a month. Expensive guitars would be rented for "many thousand dollars" every month without being used, to the point where it would have been cheaper to buy guitars like the '59 Les Paul outright.[18]

[17] Williams, R. (2017, February 24). Musician Steve Lacy releases EP recorded entirely on an iPhone. iNews. Web: https://goo.gl/JnEKHo
[18] Cormier, R. (2014, July 8). 15 Albums That Cost a Fortune to Make. Mental Floss. Web: https://goo.gl/Xys8U3

You can understand how costs for making music were also affected by the ever-changing landscape of digital music consumption. Why would labels continue spending millions to make a record when #1 hits were being comprised of nothing much more than beefed up 8-bar GarageBand drum loops? To then mention the astronomical budgets that music videos ate up over the years would belabor the point. Back at West End, it seemed like we and many other labels like us were struggling with creating new and sustainable business models because the old models were either impermissible or simply didn't work within a digital music construct. The reason many of us priced our digital downloads higher than iTunes was because we weren't seeing a cost benefit as compared to the return on vinyl sales. 99¢ was such a paltry amount to us and when Traxsource.com launched, they offered downloads at $2.99 during the promotional period or the time in which there is the most interest garnered on a release. After they took their 40% share, it left us with a slightly higher return than iTunes anyway. So, we had to turn things up a notch. With the release of "Save a Place on the Dance Floor for Me" sung by sensational singer/songwriter Dawn Tallman, West End was hoping to take 2007 by storm. The song is co-written by music producer Warren Rigg and West End's co-founder Mel Cheren. This was the only song Mel ever wrote and released. The song has a lot of meaning to Mel as it paid homage to the over 300 friends Mel lost in the fight against AIDS. The lyrics are a bit of a tear-jerker and with Dawn's soulful rendition, I usually have a hard time listening without choking up.

To help properly promote the release, we hired a big music marketing firm that specialized in national club promotion and mix show radio airplay. We purchased a CD duplicator and followed the firm's directions to commission a few different remixes of the song to appeal to different genres. We then made several dozen CD copies that were then mailed around the country. The mailing list was comprised of top 40 radio DJs, Billboard magazine reviewers, reporters and tastemakers. In this context, being able to distribute our own music on iTunes (our faux nemesis) was a huge benefit. This audience didn't purchase their digital music from West End's website nor from Traxsource.com. They downloaded their songs from iTunes. In the short term, the investment seemed to work. Dawn Tallman's "Save a Place on the Dance Floor for Me" spent 14 weeks on the Billboard dance charts and peaked at #18.[19]

I felt like we were smart to use this Billboard chart position as a big marketing tool for the song, but it was a lot of work for the label. With a staff of seven and a rigorous release schedule to maintain, we sent out several targeted email blasts, hosted big club events, had Dawn perform fast and slow versions of the song (depending on the occasion), had street teams in place to hand out flyers, launched a weekly DJ dance party in New York City's meatpacking district and more. While all of this wasn't done solely in support of one release, it was all done in the spirit of turning things up a notch. In the long term, however, the release was a fiscal loss for West End. It wasn't because the song wasn't good (it was); I think we simply misunderstood and miscalculated the changing digital landscape around us. West End spent thousands and only saw a slight bump in sales during the initial release

[19] Chart History. (2006, December 9). Save A Place On The Dance Floor For Me Promo Only: Underground Club (January 2007). Billboard. Web: http://www.billboard.com/artist/300537/dawn-tallman/chart

period. This is crucial because after the initial interest wanes, sales only go down from there. Outside of the rare exception, all of our songs were most profitable during the first two or three weeks of their release. After that point, the digital income decreased quickly over time and we were astonished. To combat this, we developed an *all in* approach to digital sales. The thought was that if we had more digital stores that carried our music, the better off we'd be. It was the very approach West End took with physical music stores. In his autobiography, Mel recounts a story of his time as salesman for ABC/Paramount Records. Mel would travel across sections of the country visiting stores and volunteering to dress their store windows with swag and products. He also kept in touch with store managers and developed relationships that increased the bottom line. In the digital realm, however, we were completely unmatched. West End signed a digital distribution deal to aggregate our entire catalog to over 200 stores at once. Before we knew it, West End's music was available at almost any digital download site you could search on the Internet.

It's also important to mention that during this period, a lot of our income was tied up in production. For vinyl to hit the market, there are upfront costs that, when multiplied by several vinyl orders at once, can quickly create a huge deficit.

And then, there was the cat and mouse game that I often played with vinyl distributors. Most vinyl distributors we dealt with agreed to terms where they paid on all vinyl copies *sold* after 120 days. At 120 days, I'd call the distributor to inquire about payment and would usually be informed of breakages and returns. In lieu of payment, vinyl distributors would use these breakages and returns as currency by reducing the balance owed to reflect their reported losses. This also bought them more time before finally remitting payment in full. This is another classic example of the failure of manual interplay as I discussed earlier. Sometimes, 180 days would pass before we'd see any real income. This, multiplied by a hectic *two records a month* release schedule, spelled fiscal disaster in the long term. I learned that you can't put all of your label's *eggs* into one or two *baskets*. It was too risky. We had depended too heavily on a hit to come or a strong reorder on a release. We also had staff salaries, an office in pricey Manhattan, merchandise costs, the added costs of starting a new weekly nightclub venture and more. We kept the spirit of West End Records alive by also hosting huge throwback parties with a featured disco headliner. We booked hugely talented performers like Jocelyn Brown and France Joli, and with Mel at the center of it all, it all felt right and respectful. In support of West End's new music, we tried hosting 'in store' events at Virgin Megastore, announced online sales discounts, and even started a printed magazine. In fact, you're reading this book right now because of that printed magazine. Sadly, *Listen Magazine* only circulated two issues, but it was during this process that I began writing about what I was noticing in the music business, especially around digital downloads. Here's an article I wrote for the magazine's first issue, published in the spring of 2006:

> Beginning in the new millennium, house music industry insiders started to feel that vinyl and CD sales were on the decline, but no one could figure out why.

Major record companies continuously blamed piracy (including illegal downloading) and proceeded to apply security protection on purchased CDs (via copy-protected products) and caused more problems than resolutions as a result. Some consumers complained that the same CDs they purchased weren't playable on computers, while others complained that stand-alone CD players also did not allow CDs to simply play, let alone copy/rip.

In 2006, insiders are faced with a new reality beyond copy-protected CDs: digital downloads. At its inception, major record companies again voiced serious concerns about the popularization of digital downloads and its subsequent demise of tangible products, such as CDs, DVDs and vinyl. Contrary to what we've been hearing for the past three years, the music business is still in very good shape today. The problem is with the record industry and CD sales. The Big-4 major label groups-- Sony BMG, Universal Music Group, EMI and Warner-- are all suffering. But if one looks beyond CD sales, it is clear that, overall, the music market is vibrant and alive. More music has been enjoyed over the past two years than ever before. However, things are going to get a lot worse for the record companies and for music stores and CD retailers, in particular. As of 2003, overall "record" (CD) sales were down 26 percent from their peak in 2000, and the total revenue is down some $2 billion.[20]

---

[20] Kusek, D. (2005). The Future of Music: Manifesto for a Digital Music Revolution 10: 6-7, 31. Boston: Berklee Press.

Major companies took notice at the way downloads were slowly becoming an integral part of pop culture, especially with the birth of Apple's portable digital music device — the iPod. iTunes gave the opportunity for major companies to partner with Apple and enjoy the benefits of an alternate revenue stream that was set apart from CD sales and they jumped on the iTunes bandwagon. Most digital downloads purchased on the iTunes system are offered at 99¢ per track. As a result, a quagmire quickly developed between the major-4 labels and iTunes because iTunes' pricing model was short-sighted and has made it extremely difficult for these same companies to enjoy healthy financial growth in terms of digital sales in the future.

Singles have never been even remotely profitable for the recording artist, and the new pay-per-track online models sported by iTunes, Rhapsody, BuyMusic, and others will ultimately fare no better. Apple reports that some of the iTunes downloads are for complete album packages, at album prices, but it will be very difficult to keep digital album prices at $10-$12 when the novelty wears off. The bottom line is that selling the content is very unlikely to be the main method of bringing revenue to the coffers of digital music services. What can we, within the dance music community, learn from this? More importantly, how can small independent companies keep business afloat and maintain relevance in the market?

While major labels have partnered with very few companies (iTunes, Rhapsody, BuyMusic, and Yahoo Music so far), small dance music companies have started to forge partnerships with multiple download websites, thus creating less of a financial dependence on any one company.

Beyond digital download sales, smaller companies can maximize the business opportunities afforded to them via their own website by manufacturing other non-CD and non-vinyl goods, such as merchandise and apparel and even ringtones, another digital product that is gaining speed in terms of popularity.

One thing is for certain, in the coming years, if it's not digital downloads or ringtones, digitally accessible products will remain popular and easier for the consumer.[21]

I laugh a little at my writing style back then, but I thank you for obliging me this trip down memory lane. While the article certainly could've been written better, I'm proud that I was able to see some of the issues arising back then that are so ever-present today. In retrospect, I think I was correct in stating that small labels need not put all of their proverbial *eggs* in one basket. Aggregating your music to many download websites is short-sighted without a robust strategy. If you're a small record label, it's essential that you find where your digital audience exists. Sometimes, they exist mostly on two or three sites and you may not learn that until you've aggregated your material to dozens

[21] Cruz, A. (2006). The Future of House Music: Digitizing the Global Dance Floor. New York: Listen Magazine.

of sites. The key that I failed to mention in that 2006 piece was that there needs to be an assessment period where the data about your digital sales can be examined and a way forward forged, based on that analysis.

Once we looked at the numbers, it was clear that West End's digital audience was on Traxsource, Beatport, West End's own website, and iTunes, in that order. But we had the entire catalog available on more than 200 online stores. Instead of scaling way back, we let the material live online arguing that if someone discovered West End on a site we don't know and then buys something of ours, then that's a good thing because it didn't cost us anything more and our share of that purchase would trickle back to us. Again, we were operating from a *vinyl* mindset where upfront costs were a regular occurrence. In doing that though, we completely ignored the biggest issue which was that, indeed, there *was* a cost. I argue that the cost of being overly accessible meant that West End's music was now devalued. We were supposed to be the brand of class and distinction, but in a digital flash, we were just like everyone else, wading in the muck and mire while hoping for a click. buy. download. So, as I mentioned earlier, there were three glaring mistakes made during this time by West End and the wider music business. The first was our inability to see that making West End's catalog overly available digitally caused a devaluation of its music. The second mistake was allowing West End to be at the mercy of one or two vinyl distributors. Much like the online store analogy I mentioned earlier, too much of our cash was being held up by one or two distributors or one or two releases or one or two new artist signings. Take your pick. A major hit or a major flop felt like it could cripple us financially.

Everything seemed to hang in the balance and on the verge. In reality, we were at a tipping point—that pivotal moment that Malcolm Gladwell talked about. West End was at a threshold, a precipice.

The third mistake was underappreciating the fact that digital piracy was our biggest threat and in large part, piracy explained why we weren't enjoying a higher profit margin. To his credit, Mel seemed to always find out when someone illegally manufactured vinyl copies of West End's music or illegally used the logo from famed NYC nightclub The Paradise Garage. It was a trademark that Mel owned after all. Vinyl bootleggers had been around for decades and this issue felt like a losing battle or a swim upstream. Given all that we were undertaking, how could we find the time to play *search and destroy* with illegal bootleggers? What would we gain by doing this? It was too easy for us to simply throw our hands up and shrug away the flagrant digital piracy that was occurring on the Internet. Furthermore, overexposing ourselves online made it extremely easy for illegal pirates to freely download West End's entire catalog. What could we do to stop it, especially considering the music industry's subpar responses and misdirected efforts?

Luckily for us, we weren't the only industry severely affected by the rise and subsequent expansion of illegal piracy. We just weren't doing anything about it. It can't go unnoticed that record labels allowed tech giants like Apple to dictate how we were going to make money from digital music, but in the nightmare that is illegal piracy, Apple did not provide any substantive help on the matter.

Unsurprisingly, software company Microsoft has been fighting the good fight and the music business (by doing nothing) has benefited. In November 2010, *The New York Times* published an article entitled "Chasing Pirates: Inside Microsoft's War Room" that details Microsoft's expensive efforts to fight pirates. It's the kind of piece that while reading it, you'll wish you had remembered the popcorn. I don't mind if you put this book down for a few minutes while you pop some popcorn before reading an excerpt from the article:

> As the sun rose over the mountains circling Los Reyes, a town in the Mexican state of Michoacán, one morning in March 2009, a caravan of more than 300 heavily armed law enforcement agents set out on a raid. All but the lead vehicle turned off their headlights to evade lookouts, called "falcons," who work for La Familia Michoacana, the brutal Mexican cartel that controls the drug trade. This time, the police weren't hunting for a secret stash of drugs, guns or money. Instead, they looked to crack down on La Familia's growing counterfeit software ring. The police reached the house undetected, barreled in and found rooms crammed with about 50 machines used to copy CDs and make counterfeit versions of software like Microsoft Office and Xbox video games. They arrested three men on the spot, who were later released while the authorities investigate the case. "The entire operation was very complicated and risky," says a person close to the investigation, who demanded anonymity out of fear for his life.

The raid added to a body of evidence confirming La Familia's expansion into counterfeit software as a low-risk, high-profit complement to drugs, bribery and kidnapping. The group even stamps the disks it produces with "FMM," which stands for Familia Morelia Michoacana, right alongside the original brand of various software makers. The cartel distributes the software through thousands of kiosks, markets and stores in the region and demands that sales workers meet weekly quotas, this person says, describing the operation as a "form of extortion" on locals. The arrival of organized criminal syndicates to the software piracy scene has escalated worries at companies like Microsoft, Symantec and Adobe. Groups in China, South America and Eastern Europe appear to have supply chains and sales networks rivaling those of legitimate businesses, says David Finn, Microsoft's anti-piracy chief. Sometimes they sell exact copies of products, but often peddle tainted software that opens the door to other electronic crime. "As long as intellectual property is the lifeblood of this company, we have to go protect it," Mr. Finn says. Microsoft has adopted a hardline stance against counterfeiting. It has set up a sophisticated anti-piracy operation that dwarfs those of other software makers; the staff includes dozens of former government intelligence agents from the United States, Europe and Asia, who use a host of "CSI"-like forensic technology tools for finding and convicting criminals. . ."[22]

---

[22] Vance, A. (2010, November 6). Chasing Pirates: Inside Microsoft's War Room. New York Times. Web:
http://www.nytimes.com/010/11/07/technology/07piracy.html

That riveting story about Microsoft's attempt at fighting software piracy always stayed with me. Until this piece was published, I had no idea how hard software companies worked to protect their products from pirates. Also, I couldn't help but connect the dots between Microsoft's story and our own music business. I've already discussed how the music business let tech companies take the lead with digital music. After reading the Microsoft article, I realized how little the music business fought to protect its music from pirates and oftentimes, their own crooked customers.

In recent years, the RIAA has been heralded for its fight against their latest piracy threat—stream ripping. For a long time, certain apps and sites let users turn streamed songs into MP3s. My buddy Eddie often reminds me of when *Real Player* was popular at the turn of the millennium. He remembers how easy it was to convert what you were hearing online into a downloadable file. We're talking circa 1998 here. Fast forward to the summer of 2017 and the Recording Industry Association of America settles its lawsuit against YouTube-mp3.org, one of the biggest stream ripping sites in the world. It was simple to use. Copy and paste the link from a YouTube video into the YouTube-mp3 site's engine and it converted the link into a downloadable MP3. Don't get me wrong. I'm not at all suggesting that the RIAA shouldn't have initiated a lawsuit against YouTube-mp3. Their platform made it easy for anyone to engage in flagrant copyright infringement. However, when you look into the RIAA's practices around the piracy battle, you'll realize the spotty track record they've had.

Look no further than their attempts to arrest young people during the peer-to-peer scandal I discussed earlier.

Is the RIAA the music industry's version of Microsoft in terms of the piracy battle? I say no!

Stream ripping isn't going anywhere. The fact also remains that piracy isn't going anywhere either. Take the Aeolian Company for example. Some of our earliest instances of piracy in the U.S. can be traced back to the player piano of the late 19th and early 20th centuries. The player piano became popular because of the self-playing mechanism that allowed pianos to play music on their own. The player piano read and played music notes from a type of perforated paper or metal sheet. It read and played the popular music of the day. Wanting to corner the market as the biggest manufacturer of the player piano, Aeolian began mass producing player pianos and securing exclusive licenses to have music already included inside each of their pianos only. They simply made the music available by pairing it with a product exclusively. The problem was in the exclusivity. Competitors of the player piano couldn't compete with Aeolian. After all, how well can you sell a player piano that doesn't have any popular music to read and play from? So, Congress stepped in to create what is known as a *compulsory license*, which allowed for competition. As it turns out, the lack of competition during this time is what caused piracy to take root. Why? Because demand didn't meet supply in the market. So piracy filled in the gap. Pirating was also known as *bootlegging*, a term coined during prohibition in the U.S. when the illegal transporting of liquor was prevalent aboard ships.

Liquor would be hidden inside boot tops, a part of the ship's body known as a *hull*. Traffickers during this time were called *bootleggers*. In the end, what was it that stopped bootlegging? It wasn't the never-ending fight against criminal activities on the high seas. It wasn't the government spending millions of dollars to clamp down on illegal trafficking. They did and it didn't stop. It wasn't even the legalization and regulation of alcohol in 1933. In 1933, the 21st Amendment to the Constitution was passed and ratified, but this ultimately ended prohibition, not bootlegging. Piracy simply took on other forms after that. It didn't cease to exist. In the case of the Aeolian Company, it was Congress that stopped their misconduct by creating that 1909 compulsory license. That certainly helped. The RIAA stopping YouTube-mp3 in 2017? That certainly helped. Microsoft spends millions and creates anti-piracy task forces. That certainly helps them. It helps the music business too.

At a basic level, Microsoft, in rooting out software piracy, is inadvertently fighting the good music piracy fight for us. Beyond this, Microsoft's efforts teach us to realize how dedicated we can become towards protecting our music and improving the way we as artists get paid for our work. We need a game changer that stops music piracy in its tracks. If you ask some people, streaming did just that. Others think that piracy persists and will never cease to exist.

As all of this was happening, I again prepared to send the next round of royalty statements to our artists and pay them.

Chapter 4: Mel was Mel Until the End

You have to admit that streaming completely changed music. What a powerfully impactful thing to have occurred. This wasn't like vinyl or a cassette tape or a Walkman or a CD. Streaming media was the colossal shift we underappreciated and we were ill-equipped to handle. In my little niche market bubble, streaming was thought of as a way to audition songs before buying them. West End edited full songs into thirty second snippets and allowed potential customers to audition each song before purchase. We were following the lead of iTunes and Traxsource, after all. When you think about it, this was our first foray into streaming media. We looked at it as a means to an end. Audition the song for thirty seconds and you'll click. buy. download. Unbeknownst to us, our biggest competitors weren't other similar record labels nor piracy. Our biggest competitor would come in the form of a full length stream and would be absolutely FREE to access.

Personally, I was a newlywed, a new home owner and feeling good about my own life, but our family was also dealing with the slow deterioration of my step-father who was battling Parkinson's and Alzheimer's. He passed away on December 13, 2005. 2006 flew by in a flash. Sarah and I learned we were pregnant, but then miscarried shortly thereafter. It was a devastating blow. The ups and downs of 2006, I learned, were a preview of what was to come.

As I mentioned, we planned to take the industry by storm at West End. It just wasn't the kind of storm we had in mind. In fact, I think it destroyed us as a work group. When I think about it: there was a duality happening at West End—a *push/pull* force at play between the old sounds of the famed Paradise Garage nightclub and the new sounds of global nightlife in the 21st century. There was also a *push/pull* force in terms of the label's legacy. Mel's legacy, in particular, made us ponder whether the label was gay or straight. I know it's strange to apply a sexuality to a record label, but hear me out. Mel, being a gay activist and pioneer, was always concerned about continuing to bring awareness to the LGBTQ community. To that end, he signed material from openly gay artists to further that awareness. Our other releases as well as the new direction for the label felt like a counterbalance to Mel's efforts. In one instance, he purchased the rights to preacher Carl Bean's gay anthem, "I Was Born This Way." In another instance, he had us arrange for West End to produce director Joseph Lovett's soundtrack for his documentary, "Gay Sex in the 70s." However, many of our supporters and patrons are straight, so therefore, we couldn't ignore the wide diversity of our buying audience. From a business perspective, the system we developed over time at West End really gave the illustrious label the best chance it had at succeeding as a modern incarnation. That meant that Mel signed certain material and we signed others. As you can imagine, manual interplay is an unintended consequence to a solidly developed system. Let me give you an example of what I mean. In its heyday, West End could rely on a trifecta of circumstances that provided success and fame for the label. Back then, the record label, the night club and the radio station all played a synergistic role in the success of a record.

With this perfect storm at work, you gave your new song the best chance at a hit it had, but any good system needed good people to work it back then. In New York City, we had the pleasure of Frankie Crocker, a WBLS on-air personality, whose broadcasts were infectious as much as they were influential. It was common that a new song, played by Paradise Garage DJ Larry Levan one Saturday night, would drive sales at the record store the next day and into the next week. Frankie would stop by the Garage on a Saturday and by Monday that hot new song would be played on the radio. All of it drove sales for that record label. It happened at West End Records many times during this period. Songs like Loose Joints' "Is It All Over My Face," Taana Gardner's "Heartbeat" and Peech Boys' "Don't Make Me Wait" became smash singles, thanks to this trifecta of synergy occurring. By 2007 and in sharp contrast, West End no longer had a 'Frankie Crocker' figure at the radio station. By this point, most of the relatable radio stations in New York had long gone, along with the Paradise Garage, Frankie Crocker, Larry Levan and *all* of the neighboring record stores—Virgin Megastore, Tower Records, Vinylmania, Satellite Records, Dance Tracks and Disco-O-Rama. All gone. Next came the realization that we were spending more money than we were taking in. Our last project cost nearly $25K and had only brought in less than $5K. We started arguing more and more about what to do and it became clear that I was not in any real decision-making position. Seeing the writing on the wall, I resigned. Exactly one month later, the partnership at West End dissolved.

The biggest hit in the storm came when Mel Cheren—our Godfather of Disco—broke the news that he had contracted HIV and now had full blown AIDS.

I felt sucker-punched, like I lost complete air in my lungs. Mel could be grouchy and moody, but like a loved one, I loved him like newly discovered family. I also regarded Mel as my musical mentor. After my step-father's passing, my mother sold our childhood home, began a new relationship, and moved to Texas, arriving on December 26, 2006. In 2007, she gave my sister and me some money as a gift from our late step-father. I took that money and bought a midi controller, a microphone and stand, a computer, and a digital audio workstation (DAW) via Pro Tools, an application software used for recording, editing and producing audio files. I didn't know what I was doing, but I got right to work anyway.

Since the dissolution, Mel needed help managing the part of the catalog that he retained. He called me and asked me to come back and manage *the classics*. So I did. I came back, on a part-time basis, to help him close out outstanding business matters. I would meet him at his spacious Manhattan duplex. At first glance, the architectural beauty took my breath away especially because I had never stepped foot inside a duplex until I entered Mel's. It was huge! The location alone would make any real estate mogul drool with the possibilities. Mel's home took up two floors of a bed and breakfast he founded decades earlier. The building sat in the middle of a picturesque block lined with beautiful brick face brownstones throughout, so standing out amongst the others was quite a task for the Colonial House Inn. What made it stand out was the curb appeal and its rich history. The steps are adorned with oversized potted plants, a gorgeous set of huge double doors made of oak and both Rainbow and American flags.

I was always intrigued by the statement that these two flags, hanging side by side, made about Mel. While he was fiercely pro LGBTQ, he was also just as patriotic. Mel voted . . . for everything. He voted in all elections, helped spread the word about the power of voting and criticized politicians when they screwed up. My intrigue laid in the dichotomy that existed in what those flags represented in Mel's life. This was a man that wrote about the *Stonewall* riots and gay liberation not only because he lived through it, but because he experienced his own country not supporting his community while completely ignoring the developing AIDS epidemic.

He lived at the Colonial House Inn on West 22nd Street, the epicenter of it all.

When you entered the Colonial House, you'd immediately be met with the aroma of coffee brewing in the lobby area. The coffee was brewed daily and served with a hint of cinnamon which I loved. There were special details paid attention to. From the outside to the hallways inside, everything felt cozy, intelligent and artistic. The white walls throughout the twenty guest rooms and two family suites always displayed beautiful art that taught as it inspired you. Walking through the front doors, past the lobby and straight down the hallway to the end, you encountered yet another set of double doors. This is where Mel lived. I usually knocked and then heard him call out to come in. His duplex was usually dimly lit with Mel usually nowhere in sight. Much like his life, his space was interesting, inspiring and creative. His walls were decorated with music awards, West End swag and Paradise Garage memorabilia. He was also a collector of paintings as well as being a painter himself. So, there was always something to look at: a quilt from the AIDS Memorial Quilt Project, a rare piece from Keith Haring, and his Billboard Trendsetter and GMHC awards. Dark wooden floors with high ceilings, a spiral staircase to the bottom floor and a gorgeous outdoor patio made it its own paradise.

Being charged with managing the West End classics meant that I spent a lot of time in the basement of the Colonial House and nowhere near that beautiful outdoor patio. Mel kept catalog-related materials, merchandise, paperwork and shipping supplies in a section of the basement shared with housekeeping staff. I'd be taking inventory trying to sort out whether he had any signed paperwork, any studio session parts and any vinyl copies left of say, Loose Joints, while the washer and dryer cycled through the day and stifled me with heat. From the basement, I'd manage vinyl re-orders, follow up on unpaid balances due to us from distributors and watch Mel deteriorate quickly that year in 2007. It got so bad that he could no longer stay in that beautiful West 22nd Street duplex. He was withering away and I felt tremendously sad and ill-equipped. One night after visiting him while in hospice care, he was completely out of it. He didn't recognize anyone, barely moved and stopped speaking. I just talked to him and told him how much he meant to me and how much he taught me and how much I appreciated him. I cried and left there feeling disoriented and angry at how this could happen to a man who fought so tirelessly against AIDS.

I was walking back towards the train that night, headed home. Horns blared annoyingly and the wind and harsh sounds of the traffic going by only added to the merciless feeling of the world at that time.

On my way down the block, I ran into Will Socolov, a longtime friend of Mel's and the co-founder of another famed record label, Sleeping Bag Records (a favorite of mine). He offered me a ride to the station and comforted me with conversation and encouraging words. It's funny how a simple conversation could conjure up so many emotions. I couldn't even tell you what we talked about and it doesn't even matter. He was a voice of calm in a storm.

I couldn't stop thinking about Mel, Warren and Dawn's record "Save a Place on the Dance Floor for Me." The more I thought about it, the more it seemed to be a clarion call from Mel to his dearly departed friends. He was requesting that a space be saved for him because he was going to be joining them soon. I didn't quite get the meaning of the latter part of that statement until later.

When I hear our songs play / Close my eyes and see your smiling face / They are still in my mind / All songs bring me back to Paradise... Save a place on the dance floor for me / Moments etched in my memory / The time we shared / How much I cared for you / Save a place for me.

Mel Cheren passed away on December 7, 2007.

Chapter 5: Life after Death

2008 was a strange year both personally and professionally. Admittedly, I was in a haze for a while. I felt lost without my professional mentor. My own father passed away on December 17th and while his passing happened twenty-three years earlier, I couldn't help but ponder whether a connection existed between Mel, my dad and the pattern of mourning during the month of December in my own life. Mel wasn't a father-figure to me, but the intense learning that occurred by working at West End with him created a bond that isn't unlike the way we bond with family, I think.

Mel's memorial service was odd. I was feeling so selfish. Everyone seemed to be called up to speak about Mel, but to me, no one was around in the year leading up to his death. I was there and I certainly felt deserving of being invited to speak at his memorial service. Winter was in its brutally coldest form and I was feeling especially icy. Thankfully, my wife Sarah was there and was a source of true comfort during this time. She let me feel how I felt without passing judgement and her warmth calmed me. We walked into Saint Peter's Lutheran Church at 54th Street and Lexington Avenue and barely found seating in a packed house of attendees that evening on January 17, 2008. Saint Peter's is an architectural icon, a massive structure founded by a group of German immigrants in 1862. The church, along with its famous organ, was created as a work of art, designed visually and tonally to fit the sanctuary, but I didn't notice any of it. The service included a eulogy from one of West End's legendary artists, Taana Gardner, along with a who's who in disco and dance music. It was beautiful and touching, but in that moment, I felt so foolish. The stories each person told just reaffirmed my respect and appreciation for Mel, but all of them had decades of association with him. I worked for him during the last three years of his life. They were all deeply rooted friends and colleagues for more than thirty or forty years. Why did I expect to be included? I just cried. I was crying over the loss of a dear colleague, but I was also sobbing about my own selfishness.

Two things happened to me that night. Yes, I was definitely forced to let go of my selfishness and confront the loss of my work colleague, but I was also inspired. During the service, the stories of what Mel did to keep music alive or to let the world know that people were dying of AIDS felt deeply profound. Living and dying are the bookends, but what are the books of your life? What will you leave behind that helps someone else? When I really examined myself, I realized that working at West End felt like being a part of dance music royalty. Anyone who is tuned into these creative communities would agree. Mel made me feel like I wasn't just an employee, but a part of his family. He was loyal to me and I wanted a chance to say how much he meant to me, but I didn't need a crowd of mourners to express that. Each one of the speakers during the service recalled so many moments where Mel showed his devotion to them or to a cause and with each new eulogy, my selfishness converted to shame (for being so foolish), and then converted again to inspiration.

You see, inspiration isn't just a feeling or a sense that perhaps, you could accomplish what you haven't, but it's actually the fuel that drives the car that contains your dreams. Dreams travel. Even right at this moment, you can begin dreaming about something you've always wanted to accomplish and you'll notice that you might naturally look upward or outward as you daydream. You might even sense that your dreams are somewhere above you or in front of you, just out of reach. It's no surprise that we often look up or look out while daydreaming. This seems to be our brain's way of visualizing what's to come with action. Actions are the steps we must take to make our dreams come true because otherwise, what are dreams without actions?

To me, songs are dreams with actions taken. They are ideas, inspired by life, that have traveled until a point where manifestation occurs. Songs also contain healing properties and therefore, can act as therapy. The legacy of Mel Cheren is the story of what one person did to make the world change and become better.

The rest of 2008 flew by in a flash. My wife and I decided to open our home to become foster parents. We felt compelled after learning just how many children were in the social services system where we live. Also, we knew a couple who had fostered before (and recommended it) and yet another couple who was planning on becoming foster parents around the same time as us. Personally, it was a difficult time.

As I mentioned earlier, we had already gotten pregnant, had shared the good news with all of our friends and family, only to miscarry shortly thereafter. While this was obviously a devastating experience, it somehow also helped to propel us forward in taking the first steps.

There was quite a process involved. Social Services required us to take several parenting classes over a 6 week span. They also conducted background checks, home inspections, interviews and more.

Once our house officially became licensed, we were told to expect the placement calls to come in at any time. From our classes, we already knew that we'd likely be asked to take in several children at once (usually siblings), but we thought we'd just decline until only one child was made available to us.

Our very first call came on December 26, 2008, the day after Christmas. We were asked to take in two sisters, ages one and two. We were told that their placement with us was temporary and would only last for two months. We almost immediately said yes despite our 'one child' agreement and set off to pick up a bunch of stuff in preparation for their arrival: diapers, clothes of various sizes, supplies, cribs, bedding and so much more. It was like those timed shopping spree game shows where you have five minutes to buy as many products as possible.

Tamirah and Seyoni arrived after 6 pm that same evening. They were seven months and nineteen months, respectively (not exactly one and two years old). Two months turned into six months and six months turned into forever.

They've been with us ever since.

The years, while extremely rewarding, were filled with once-a-month visits from case workers, nurses, resource workers and law guardians. There were several court dates, trials and legal hurdles to overcome and many weekends visiting with their biological family, committing ourselves to keeping the relationship open. As their Dad, I immediately regarded them as my own children. To me, they even resembled us and so, adoption was a no-brainer. No other option has ever occurred to me.

Until the legal decisions came, there was a lot of speculation. One month, we were told that they'd never be placed out of our home. Another month, we were told to expect the worst and that there was a chance they may not stay with us. These uncertainties were the hardest part of the process, to be honest. Would they stay with us forever? Would they be taken from us abruptly? What's best for them? If they did have to leave us, how can we make the transition as smooth as possible for them? What's taking so long?

We asked ourselves these questions often and it became very stressful on all of us. I think that asking questions and being communicative with social services (and everyone involved) helped to deal with the stress of the uncertainties. We stayed on top of the case and kept asking for updates and follow-ups to the point of exhaustion. As time passed on, we resolved to take care of them while they were in our home and we had faith. We also learned that we were expecting our own child and couldn't believe what was happening!

We were away at a family wedding in Vermont when we got the call that we were weeks away from final adoption. Sarah was eight months pregnant at the time. We just cried and hugged each other. It felt like we had come to the finish line of a long race and discovered that we had won. I watched my daughters swim and play in beautiful Lake Eden that day and felt like our lives were just beginning.

We finally adopted our daughters on August 1, 2012. Our son AJ arrived two days later. In one week, we officially became parents of three children!

2008 was obviously a pivotal year for me personally, but my professional life was taking me down a new road. I tinkered away at producing new music throughout the rest of 2007 and by February, I was ready to release my own music. I launched my own record label, Mixtape Sessions, but before it became a record label, Mixtape Sessions was a radio style mix show that operated in Brooklyn at Halcyon. Halcyon was the kind of place that was truly unique. It was a coffee-shop, eatery, record store, furniture store and chill out spot, all in one. The original Mixtape Sessions was co-founded by Lola Rephann of Deep See fame, in October 1999. It was Lola who thought of the name after hearing my description of a mixed set idea I had. I had always wanted to collaborate with other DJs. We had our first 'session' in October and then afterwards, Lola thought we could create a regular thing out of it. We got together again in December of 1999 and Mixtape Sessions was born! Lola remained my co-host until leaving the show to pursue graduate studies and other work ambitions. I kept it going and continued inviting other DJs to come record a mix show with me. I started interviewing them as part of the session and recorded most of them. Today, you can hear some of my interviews with such talents as: Anané Vega, Louie Vega, Jellybean Benitez, Tony Humphries, Mr. V, Alix Alvarez, and so many others on my website at mixtapesessions.com

On February 28, 2008, Mixtape Sessions released the *Overcome* EP, a four-track collection featuring my sister, Flora Cruz, as the main artist. Flora would bring her journal to our recording sessions and we would convert some of those journal entries into song lyrics. These lyrics were heartfelt and profound, chronicling a woman's journey of self-discovery, empowerment and triumph over adversity. To boot, we had a modest hit on our hands with "Let the Sunshine Out," a song about breaking out of your shell and letting your inner light shine. Folks love Flora's singing. Her voice reminds people of Latina singers Lisa Lisa and La India, but Flora's vocals are a style all her own. She is endearing, truthful and sassy. I did the best I could knowing little to nothing about producing music, but doing it anyway. The proof that I didn't know what I was doing is in those initial Mixtape Sessions releases. For example, I recorded all of Flora's initial vocals with the microphone turned around, so I captured Flora's performances using the back of the microphone when it should've been front facing. Despite that, the sessions were a lot of fun. We often recorded with family members and close friends, many of whom are talented themselves. Cousins sang background vocals during the "Let the Sunshine Out" sessions and provided percussion on songs like "Raise It Up," and friends would sing on songs like "No Regrets." It was a family affair and it was healing and it kept me busy. I had to recall all of the skills I acquired at other labels and apply them to my own and there was so much to do.

I had to consider and constantly work at website design, promotions, marketing, producing, DJing and trying to keep making money now that I was essentially unemployed. All in the span of a few months, I signed the phenomenal singer and performer Manchildblack, released his four track *My Mind's I* EP, finished Flora's debut album, released her eleven track *Dulce Melodia* LP, and collaborated with another fantastic singer and performer Eddie Nicholas, releasing his single entitled "Ghumbah," all while commissioning and later releasing remixes on two more singles for Flora. I worked at a frenetic pace, launching an Internet radio show which broadcasted the recordings from the old Halcyon sessions as well as new mix shows. Unbeknownst to me, I was unintentionally building a brand and developing a reputation for airing quality dance music mix shows on the web. I just knew that I had these incredible recordings and I knew people would enjoy hearing me DJ alongside other great DJs and then interviewing them. I would ask about their musical beginnings, their thoughts on the current state of affairs in the music business and their future plans. It was more than just a mix show.

I was asked to manage a website for a huge recording facility in the Ironbound section of Newark, New Jersey. When you drive down McCarter Highway and make a left on South Street, you'll cross a desolate area of the city that transforms before your eyes. As you continue down the block, the landscape will change from homes to restaurants to industrial complexes to a major highway that leads to the airport. If you ignore the Eye of Horus on the front door, you could easily drive past the monstrous, yet mysterious looking building on Jefferson Street painted completely in black.

Axiom Studios was a full-scale recording facility with DJ equipment, a DJ booth and a broadcasting setup that was quite impressive. It also contained an oversized dance space, wooden floors, a top notch PA system, and a large recording studio. In its heyday, Axiom equipped several of the rooms with recording equipment when their session work was in high demand. My job was to maintain their active website by uploading each broadcast and sharing the archive links on the site, managing the broadcasts at the facility, and helping to welcome and orient new broadcasters.

From my work at Axiom, I was recommended for additional part-time work, assisting the data mining initiatives of an Information Technology doctor and professor from Rutgers University. I was charged with troubleshooting the doctor's technology techniques and software around sentiment analysis. His IT company analyzes millions of bloggers' sentiments and attaches those sentiments to a video ad server for better segmentation. He did a bunch of other things too like helping the healthcare industry analyze the insulin needs of patients using a cell phone. I was completely blown away! Here was a man who was basically recording and tracking what people thought about . . . well . . . anything! Through my work at Axiom, we were able to apply some of the doctor's technology techniques as it related to online music consumption and DJ culture. I would test out different software scripts and report back my findings. I remember pushing for the ability to track when certain songs were being played by DJs in real time using metadata. It was a long shot at the time, but the intention was to see if we were able to trigger and track when certain songs were being streamed during a DJ set.

This was way before Shazam and way ahead of its time. The ability to identify songs using metadata meant we could also track the sentiments being shared on the web about those songs. This was all really technical stuff and I really enjoyed it, but no one was offering me full-time work nor health benefits and I needed fiscal stability as I prepared to start a family. The lack of health benefits was, in part, why I resigned from West End in the first place, before the dissolution of Mel's partnership with his business partner. As a small house music industry, we don't foster a workplace culture of health benefits and vacation time. But, it's funny how the universe works.

I got a call in the spring of 2009 that I never could have predicted. After laying dormant for over a year, West End Records had become a memory in my life. I had been producing and releasing a lot of music on my own label since Mel's passing and had already celebrated the one year anniversary of the *Overcome* EP and Mixtape Sessions when a family relative of Mel's reached out to me. He had been left the company and wanted to know if I would be interested in reviving West End. By June, I was appointed Vice President of West End Records and I was stunned! This was the last thing I expected, but I instantly felt like I wanted to pay tribute to Mel and perhaps, I could do right by West End with whatever time I was given. I knew my time serving as VP was limited because it was made clear to me that the interest was to sell the label, so reviving the label was a way to entice possible buyers. I immediately went to work populating the website with news, sending out email blasts and compiling a double tribute CD, entitled *Keep On Dancin: A Tribute to the Godfather of Disco Mel Cheren.*

It included classics like "When You Touch Me" and "Is It All Over My Face?" as well as "Save A Place On The Dancefloor for Me" and new remixes of other Mel Cheren favorites. I designed the cover art, putting together a collage of photographs of Mel with friends and fans behind a much larger photo of a young Mel in the center. I knew he would have appreciated me doing that. When he was alive, Mel published a beautiful autobiography and autographed it for me. For the tribute CD, I scanned part of Mel's autograph so that everyone could have their own autographed copy of the CD straight from the man himself. It read:

Music is the Message & Love is the Answer - Mel Cheren

On the backside, I wrote:

> This special tribute is dedicated to all of you who fully understand the power that music has in the universe. It's the one true common thread that holds us together as a human race. To Mel Cheren, the music he shared with the world, especially through West End Records, turned out to be the soundtrack of his life. As it turns out, the music he shared with us has now become the soundtrack of all of our lives today. Think about it. Recall the big moments in your life. Chances are there was a song playing in the background that attached itself to your memory and it lives there forever. When you hear that certain song, it instantly brings you back to that moment in time. Mel, thank you for the wonderful memories. Today and always, we pay homage, pay tribute and pay our respects to the original soundtrack creator, the Godfather of Disco, Mel Cheren.

Within a matter of months of my tenure, the first offer came in to buy West End. I worked with the estate to inventory the remaining catalog and prepare for acquisition. I felt strange. I was still thanking people for congratulating me on the appointment while readying the label to be sold in secret. In the end, the deal fell through and I was back to conducting business as usual again. I sold out on the tribute CDs, re-manufactured them and sold out again. In the fall of 2009, I was approached by Josh Milan, a friend and one-half of the production duo Blaze. He had recently parted ways with his producing partner and was interested in launching his solo label and asked for my help. I felt honored, humbled and strange. You see, Mel's former business partner at West End is also Josh's former producing partner and my former boss. I was bearing witness to the demise of not one, but two partnerships and I felt terrible. At the same time though, I never hesitated when Josh asked me for help. I just had a good feeling about working with Josh and what a great decision it was! Honeycomb Music was formed in April of 2010 while I was putting the finishing touches on my solo debut *Life and Times* album. To distribute other labels like Honeycomb, I formed a small digital distribution company called The Cruz Music Group which allowed me to sign and release music from other labels.

As all of this was happening, I prepared to send the next round of royalty statements to our artists and pay them. Then, the second offer came in at West End. By June of 2010, I released my album and West End Records was sold to Verse Music, a music publisher who also purchased SalSoul Records (another illustrious disco label) that same summer. To boot, Axiom Studios decided to close its doors and I was laid off from my IT job.

I was unemployed again while Josh and I began building Honeycomb, scoring our first hit with Josh's single, "Your Body," along the way. I couldn't go anywhere without hearing "Your Body" that year and I was so proud, but was way too busy to take in the accomplishment. Lesson learned: take in your accomplishments.

In my personal life, we had our hands full with our daughters and I was home alone for a decent part of the year as Sarah excelled in her professional life. It made heavy travel necessary at that time and with the little time I had left, I took on as many website design, logo design and flyer design jobs as I could handle. At one point, I designed a website for a self-published author who chronicled her life while committing credit card fraud in a book she penned in prison. I worked for a hot sauce manufacturer who specialized in novelty flavors. Our pantry was stocked with enough hot sauce to light fireworks. And then one day, I received a flyer in the mail, announcing the new semester at a small liberal arts college in town. I decided that if I was going to push our daughters towards higher education, then I better finish my bachelor's degree. I attended an 'instant decision' day and was enrolled by the fall of 2010. I transferred whatever college credits I could from Rutgers and studied music technology with full force. I finally had the opportunity to learn audio engineering, sound mixing, music theory, compression, and mastering. It couldn't have been a better fit and it couldn't have come at a better time considering the ever-changing landscape of the music business, including the brutal truth which was that music was free. And if music was now free, was there a music business left?

Chapter 6: The Only Constant is Change

By 2011, YouTube had fast become the most popular online source for music and music video content. 35 hours of video footage were being uploaded to the site every minute and over 13 million hours of footage were uploaded during that prior year, 2010. More video was uploaded every 60 days than the three major US television networks produced in 60 years. And each week, YouTube received the equivalent of 115,000 full-length feature films in uploads.[23] By 2012, 72 hours of video were uploaded to the site every minute.[24] In a matter of minutes, every release I distributed, including my second *Emospiritual Travelin* album and third *Freedom* album, as well as every Honeycomb release could be found on YouTube for free and there was little I could to do to keep up with the takedown demands. It was a losing battle and the traditional methods were completely tossed out. It simply no longer worked. We were in the midst of a social media explosion where the totality of music marketing was happening online. Offline methods like flyering, party promotions and magazine ads seemed antiquated and ineffective given the barrage of music coming out from all over the world every day, every week and every month.

---

[23] Robertson, M. (2011, April 18). 25 Jawdropping YouTube Video Facts, Figures & Statistics. TubularInsights. Web: http://tubularinsights.com/youtube-statistics
[24] Al-Greene, B. (2012, December 20). YouTube in 2012: A Year of Expansion and Experiments. Mashable. Web: https://mashable.com/2012/12/20/youtube-milestones-2012/#qh3qmoGT1Zql

The number of small labels also grew. In house music, it's hard to ignore the more than 20,000 labels that Traxsource.com says they distribute on their website.[25] Each week, Traxsource.com's biggest competitor, Beatport, says its music collection is refreshed with hundreds of exclusive tracks by the world's top electronic music artists.[26] So as a label owner and small digital music distributor, my biggest competitors were the other 20,000 labels and the hundreds of house music tracks coming out every week, but more than that, all of our music being accessible for free on YouTube was the biggest competitor of all . . . that was until Spotify came to the U.S.

A Swedish based company, Spotify officially launched in European markets in 2008 with its 'all you can eat' pricing model in place. To entice its customers, Spotify allowed its users to enjoy 10 hours of free music a month. Interviewed in July of 2011 for the *Financial Times*, Spotify co-founder Daniel Ek made Spotify's intentions clear: "Our long term goal is to get everyone in the world to use Spotify," he said.[27]

> Spotify's unique selling point is the ability to listen to its library of 15 million tracks from all the leading labels for no charge. Although other digital music services offer short free trials, none has an open-ended free service to match Spotify's.

---

[25] Staff. (2018, June 10). Traxsource is the modern home for real house music. Web: https://news.traxsource.com/about

[26] Staff. (2018, June 10). About Beatport. Beatport, LLC. Web: http://about.beatport.com/

[27] Bradshaw, T. (2011, July 14). Spotify launches in the US. Financial Times. Web: https://www.ft.com/content/0d602d7c-adf9-11e0-a2ab-00144feabdc0

In that respect, according to music analyst Mark Mulligan, Spotify "doesn't have a direct rival" in North America, where subscription music so far "hasn't been able to grow out of its niche." One reason for Spotify's prolonged delay of its US launch is some labels' fears that this free service may undercut the existing market. Pandora, the online personalized radio service with 36 million active users, could lose users to Spotify's ability to choose exactly what song they want to listen to, Mr. Mulligan said.[28]

What ensued is what has been coined "the streaming wars." Two things happened simultaneously. On the one hand, the streaming wars represent a grab for your subscription dollar by streaming music services. On the other hand, it represents a shift away from non-interactive streaming and a strong pivot towards interactive media. What do I mean?

As a subscriber, you can opt to sign up for a streaming service where you can select artists you like and genres you enjoy, but you may not select a certain song on demand. Think about services like SiriusXM, TuneIn, Live365.com and especially, the popular Pandora service. Unlike those others, Pandora is now both non-interactive and interactive. Interactive streaming is completely on demand, allowing its users to select specific content instantly. As you can imagine, non-interactive streaming pays out less in royalties than interactive streaming and services with free trials pay out less in royalties than those with premium or paid subscribers.

---

[28] Bradshaw, T. (2011, July 14). Spotify launches in the US. Financial Times. Web: https://www.ft.com/content/0d602d7c-adf9-11e0-a2ab-00144feabdc0

As of September 2018, Pandora has 6 million paid subscribers, a paltry amount as compared to Spotify, one of its main competitors.[29]

Think about what Spotify did to get ahead in the streaming wars. Spotify developed the *freemium* model, a pipeline that was created to move customers from free to premium. This was the digital version of what Columbia House wished it would have become. Remember Columbia House? In the 1980s and 90s, there was a popular mail-order CD business with a huge sales gimmick to get you to buy a CD at full price. To entice its customers, Columbia House allowed its customers to choose eight CDs for a penny so long as you promised to purchase a CD at full price. But by August 10, 2015, the owners of Columbia House filed for bankruptcy, unable to continue competing for business in a digital world.[30] With its 10 hours of free music per month model, Spotify took the Columbia House concept to new heights.

But then a question was asked that changed Spotify's plans for *freemium*: are artists getting paid while these customers are enjoying Spotify's free music service? Now, let's not get confused. Streaming services do not pay artists directly. Companies like Spotify pay record labels and music publishers who, in turn, pay the artists based on the deals they've struck.

---

[29] Allen, S. (2018, September 14). Has Pandora Stock Peaked? Market Realist. Web: https://marketrealist.com/2018/09/has-pandora-stock-peaked

[30] Hamilton, J. (2015, August 12). Columbia House Offered Eight CDs for a Penny, but Its Life Lessons Were Priceless. Slate. Web: http://www.slate.com/blogs/browbeat/2015/08/12/columbia_house_bankrupt_mail_order_cd_club_s_owner_finally_going_out_of.html

Back at home, my family was growing and I was nearing the end of my adult college life. By the spring of 2012, I was preparing to release my second album. I remember an old essay I wrote for one of my classes:

> I honestly don't know where to begin. Do I first talk about the immensely cathartic experience that the songwriting process was or do I first begin with the uncomfortably vulnerable feeling of having to sing lead vocals for the first time? The process of making *Emospiritual Travelin* first began after remembering my experience with releasing the *Life and Times* LP. My debut album was an important first step for me and helped shape my passion and dedication to music. The approach with this album was to create a feeling of traveling. To me, initially I intended to invoke feelings of physical travel, but after beginning to work on each song, I noticed that, in my music and lyrics, I wasn't traveling physically. I was traveling emotionally and spiritually. So, I began to think about themes of places I've never been to and experiences I've never had. This really helped me to better understand the direction that my album would ultimately take. With each song and with each subsequent critique, I felt more vulnerable and more insecure, but in a weird way, I also felt liberated and evolved. Songs like "Travelin" speak to a more obvious idea – my desire to travel. But as I wrote the lyrics and began recalling places I'd like to visit, I focused in on South Africa.

Currently in dance music, South Africa has become an increasingly important market. DJs who only occasionally get booked stateside find much success in other countries and especially, South Africa. This is a place I've never visited, but I have colleagues and friends who have and come back with terrific stories about how much our house music is welcomed in South Africa and that I should go immediately.

So, in creating each song, I was inspired by South Africa and infused this idea with other types of music. When I researched the house music sound in South Africa, I noticed that their style of house music was more organic. Producers there use organic-sounding synth and drum sounds, but also fuse live percussion and native languages in their music. Most striking was the fact that a lot of the music is slower in tempo. While in the U.S., house music tends to run between 125-130 BPM and even faster in terms of tempo, South Africans like their brand of house music at 120-123 BPM. I allowed this to influence the general tempo of *Emospiritual Travelin* and as you listen, you'll notice this tempo on several tracks. Creating music for this album at this tempo really made me feel closer to the rhythm of the body's actual heartbeat. I tried to tap into that as part of the roadmap for developing the groove for each song, layering sounds on top as it went on and creating a build-up and a cool off. When I was done, I felt sad and thrilled much like I felt after the *Life and Times* LP. It was fun making it, but now I have to let it go.

I plan on digitally releasing several songs as singles first and the album after that. I also intend to have certain songs remixed by other producers and release this as a package. From this experience, I hope to work on the next album and tap into a totally different genre and see what comes of it.

Everything at that time was happening at top speed. The music business, in general, seemed to be operating in much the same way, but at home I wasn't going anywhere. I was barely even seen in my own dance music circles. I just think it was too hard to manage it all, but because I was determined to finish well academically, it came at a cost in terms of the DJ and producing business I thought I was building for myself. When I mention this to close friends, I get two types of responses about it. Some say that everything happens for a reason and that I've done well with building my own Mixtape Sessions as well as West End, Honeycomb Music and others throughout the years. Others say that because there's no real money in music anymore anyway, I'm in the wrong business and should get out. Many of my musical comrades have. While I don't agree that I'm in the wrong business, I do agree that we should stop ignoring what's happening and pay special attention to the ways in which the income levels for artists have deteriorated in music over time, especially in house music. I can't tell you how many times I've heard stories of a *house music heyday* where artists were chauffeured to performances in fancy limousines and treated to top notch accommodations along with top notch income to go with it. These stories often included adventures around the world complete with world class traveling and meeting creative people "when they weren't famous yet."

It all seemed like fantasy to me because it was certainly *not* the reality of house music today. What occurred to me overtime (at least partly) was the sense that my house music friends and I were perpetuating a culture of living in the past because we participated in it. The community at large was also living in the past. The music heard and the methods for bringing people to the music were all completely outdated and unusable. In particular, club spaces have suffered a tremendous blow in terms of income levels. A wonderful piece in *Insider Magazine* explains one set of arguments.

There's a massive trend brewing in America's nightlife scene. The attendance of nightclubs and bars has been on a steady decline for the past several years. Nightclubs left and right are going out of business with several others being threatened to close their doors. There have been massive declines of profit as well as overall revenue. This trend isn't only exclusive to the United States; the UK has been experiencing a great drop in their once world-renowned nightlife as well. And who or what is to blame for all of this?

Millennials.

Who are these impactful millennials?

According to GFK, the global research firm, millennials are people who were born between the years 1977 and 1994. Being between the ages of 21 and 38, they are the target demographic for all club owners and other nightlife vendors.

These millennials are very unlike their Generation X parents considering that they are very tech savvy, entered adulthood equipped with cell phones, up to date with social media, and would certainly much rather spend money on experiences rather than material things.

Considering such preferences, millennials sound like the ideal group to be regularly enjoying themselves at various nightclubs. If this is the case, why are nightclubs and venues suffering massive declines in numbers? Millennials favor experiences over material things and nightclubs should be benefiting from that. Where are these millennials going instead?

Are millennials going to nightclubs?

Simply put, not really. Countless studies and observations have shown that millennials are not going to nightclubs the way the former Generation X did. A survey by ULI/Lachman Associates shows that only slightly more than 60% of all millennials spend time at nightclubs. Of that 60%, only 25% spend time at nightclubs more than once a month. The millennials who go to nightclubs say they mostly go for special occasions. Bachelor/bachelorette parties, seeing a specific DJ or an attending celebrity, or because they are in party capitals like NYC and Las Vegas serve as the main reasons why millennials venture into nightclubs.

Nightclubs do not have a large rate of returning millennial consumers.

Nightclub owners are finding it very difficult to keep their doors open when a large number of their clientele only stop by once in a blue moon and penny-pinch on their drink orders. It comes as no surprise that an average of 6,500 venues are closing earlier each night and not making it past their first year in business in the United States according to J.C. Diaz, the Executive Director of the Nightlife Association. To add insult to injury, the IBIS World Bar Business & Nightclub Business Industry reports that bar and nightclub revenue fell 9.3% in 2009 following The Great Recession. While other businesses are slowly rising back up from the recession's higher unemployment rates and lower consumer spending, the nightclub industry isn't following the trend. The industry is not bouncing back.[31]

And again, the years moved quickly. In May 2013, I graduated summa cum laude with a Bachelor of Arts degree in Creative Arts & Technology - Music Technology. I also enjoyed the rest of the year with my young family, secured a great work-from-home job and recorded my third album while continuing to build Honeycomb Music with Josh. By then, the label we started was in its third year of operation. From the years 2012 to 2014, there seemed to be a turning point happening in music. For the first time ever, digital music sales surpassed physical music sales and streaming was becoming king. It was a game changer.

---

[31] La Vecchia, T. (2015, October 12). Bid Farewell: Why Millennials Are Abandoning Nightclubs. Insider Magazine. Web: https://newtheory.com/bid-farewell-why-millennials-are-abandoning-the-nightclub-nightlife/

Our top grossing artists were also changing and exploring new and uncharted waters in terms of digital music marketing and much like in our small independent house music world, the old methods for bringing attention to the music were tossed out. For instance, when top-selling artist Beyoncé surprise-released her fifth self-titled studio album, the industry shook. This was unheard of in the pop world. At the time, I wrote:

> Music industry insiders continue to be baffled by Beyoncé's surprise self-titled LP. Like us, they're fascinated with the pop star's ability to circumvent the glorified "machine" of the recording industry. For her fifth studio album, there was no radio single, no promotional tour, and no publicity. Nothing. This approach goes against the grain, to say the least. After all, artists and labels have long believed that without proper marketing, extensive distribution and slow-building hype, artists don't stand a chance at earning even a livable wage.
>
> The timing of this release is also worth noting as record labels shy away from fourth quarter album releases in favor of holiday collections. Because the music market is so inundated with new releases during the holiday season, the label's marketing dollars are simply spread too thin. The move to release the project on December 13th was risky, but proved worthwhile after iTunes announced that her latest LP is the fastest selling album of all time.[32]

[32] Aguiar, L., Martens, B. (2013, March 21). Digital Music Consumption on the Internet: Evidence from Clickstream Data. Contrefaçon Riposte. Web: http://www.contrefacon-riposte.info/publications/4180-digital-music-consumption-on-the-Internet-evidence-from-clickstream-data

Given all of the tools that are seemingly necessary for artists to shine, Beyoncé ditched all of them and managed to sell 300,000 copies in the first 72 hours of her release and millions more since. When you consider niche market genres such as house music, how does Beyoncé's new album impact these smaller music markets? For years, niche market artists have released their new music with little or no fanfare. Because many artists are independent, there is no "machine" to use. This is mostly because there isn't enough money to support the release. In many cases, the artist is also "the machine." In fact, without promotional help, resources and marketing money, many artists simply opt to release their music and then strategize afterwards. Not surprisingly, many artists and labels have noticed that this approach is neither fiscally successful nor sustainable.

One of the biggest challenges all artists face is the over-saturation of the music market. While iTunes regularly reports download figures to the public (over 25 billion songs have already been downloaded on iTunes so far), niche music download sites aren't as forthcoming with their data.[33] Obtaining real numbers from popular house music download sites like Beatport and Traxsource, for example, would prove insightful at this time, but these are nearly impossible to get since they're notoriously so tight-lipped.

---

[33] Apple Press Info (2013). iTunes Store Sets New Record with 25 Billion Songs Sold. Apple, Inc. Web:
http://www.apple.com/pr/library/2013/02/06iTunes-Store-Sets-New-Record-with-25-Billion-Songs-Sold.html

Despite this, Beatport's COO Matthew Adell once referenced the site's download figures at the 2010 International Music Summit in Ibiza, Spain. In answering a question about trends in retail music for DJs, he mentioned that Beatport receives "between 7,000 and 15,000 tracks per week."[34] Interestingly enough, music consumption is at an all-time high, but music sales remain at its lowest in over a dozen years. For an artist in this genre, it is increasingly more difficult to stand out and be noticed above the rest of the 15,000 or more tracks being released per week. With or without the data, it's fairly obvious that artists in this genre are not becoming popularized enough to attract investors and sponsors to support their music over time and budgets aren't increasing enough. Moreover, the quality of their digital assets (e.g., music, artwork, and videos) is not improving fast enough over time. So, what can niche market artists learn from Beyoncé's surprise album?

• **Don't pull a "Beyoncé!"**

First, having little or no strategy doesn't work for niche market artists. Beyoncé's album has been selling very well for a number of reasons, all of which are specific to Beyoncé, her music and her fans. While there's little doubt that the success of this LP will spawn similar attempts by other popular artists in the future, we'll quickly discover that this anti-marketing strategy works for certain artists and bombs for others.

---

[34] Beatport News (2010). Becoming 'One': Anatomy of a #1 hit. Beatport.com. Web: http://news.beatport.com/blog/2010/07/06/becoming-one-anatomy-of-a-1-hit

• Content Trumps Everything!

Because tastes in music are so subjective, I'll leave you to leave your comments below as to whether Beyoncé's latest effort is good or not. However, a growing consensus among critics is that the album IS good. This certainly wasn't a project that was slapped together. In fact, in one of her 'behind the scenes' clips, the 17-time Grammy winner mentioned that she recorded over 80 songs for the project and released 14 of them. So, what's the point? Take the time to release the best music that you can. Great music is truly the catalyst and the engine.

• Get Organized!

The bigger story, actually, isn't Beyoncé's surprise album, but the organization of it. This "visual album" included 14 songs, 17 videos and an array of stunning digital assets from photographs to 'behind the scenes' clips. All of this was prepared ahead of time and released all at once.

Take the time to organize all of your promotional materials before you release your music. Your biography should be concise and up-to-date.

Your cover artwork and all photographs should look clean, clear, professional and ready for use in all file formats. Your website and your social media pages should be regularly updated and should always function correctly.

If an image, button or link isn't working for you, it probably isn't working for everyone else too.

• Share Your Creative Process and Get Personal!

While there's no rule book on what to share with current and new fans, one thing is for sure - if you want more followers and "likes," you better start sharing! Take a cue from Beyoncé and prepare your own 'behind the scenes' clips and let your audience know what it took to finish your work.

• Don't Just Sell, Engage!

Think of fans as potential new friends. The last thing someone you just met wants to hear is you asking for money. Take the time to engage with fans without asking them to buy your music first. Discuss the song's meaning or a fun fact and simply, include a link. If they click through, they'll know what to do if they're interested in buying it. Don't remind them of how to do the obvious. Before you engage, take the time to understand etiquette in social media and how best to communicate across your social media networks. Be careful! If you spam potential new supporters, you'll lose them quickly.[35]

---

[35] Cruz, A. (2014, January 2). 5 Things All House Music Artists Can Learn From Beyoncé's Surprise LP. Freedom Radio Hour. Web: http://news.freedomradiohour.com/2014/01/5-things-all-house-music-artists-can.html

The *Beyoncé* album's surprise release was the kind of indication in 2014 that everyone stopped and paid attention to. A new music business model was taking hold. With Spotify's *freemium* plans firmly intact, 2014 also became the year when we finally got an answer to the question I posed earlier about *freemium*: are artists getting paid while these customers are enjoying Spotify's free music service? The answer was no and that's all that artists needed to hear before rumors began to fly. Enter: Taylor Swift.

The mega pop star was gearing up to release her highly anticipated *1989* album on all major streaming sites, including Spotify. But, in her view, Spotify's *freemium* model was nothing but "a grand experiment." Swift told Yahoo in an interview at that time: "I'm not willing to contribute my life's work to an experiment that I don't feel fairly compensates the writers, producers, artists and creators of this music."

Taylor Swift sold nearly 1.3 million copies of her latest *1989* album in its first week on sale, giving a talking point to critics who believe that Spotify, for all its hype, is not necessary for success.

In response, Daniel Ek, Spotify's chief executive, posted a statement on Spotify's blog defending the service's business model and updating some of its crucial statistics. "Spotify has now paid $2 billion in royalties and it continues to grow quickly, with 50 million users around the world, 12.5 million of whom pay for subscriptions. All the talk swirling around lately about how Spotify is making money on the backs of artists upsets me big time," Mr. Ek wrote.

"Our whole reason for existence is to help fans find music and help artists connect with fans through a platform that protects them from piracy and pays them for their amazing work."[36]

These are the two worlds that Spotify occupied at the time. On the one hand, Spotify was the villain, just another technology company taking advantage of art, the music and the business. It was viewed as an exploiter, created from a corporate mindset. On the other hand, Spotify was viewed as a savior.

Internet piracy was thought to be an unstoppable blight on the digital market as recently as five years ago. As quickly as music, movie, and video game companies could shut down pirates and pirate sites, new ones would appear. The notorious Pirate Bay website, for example, is practically indestructible, having survived being forcibly taken down almost a dozen times. Entertainment and software companies began to foretell the end of their industries due to lost profits from piracy. All of this lead to attempts by the federal government to pass draconian Internet laws like SOPA and PIPA. These bills defined Internet criminal activities incredibly broadly and would have allowed companies to bring down sites with a single complaint, with the burden of proof passing to the allegedly infringing site. When those attempts failed, companies began to attack individual pirates and pirate enablers by bringing lawsuits against them.

---

[36] Sisario, B. (2014, November 11). Chief Defends Spotify After Snub by Taylor Swift. New York Times. Web: https://www.nytimes.com/2014/11/12/business/media/taylor-swifts-stand-on-royalties-draws-a-rebuttal-from-spotify.html

For the pirates, these lawsuits could result in enormous fines relative to the value of what they downloaded. As for the enablers, one only needs to look at the history of Napster and Megaupload to see how far these companies were willing to go to stop illegal downloads. Napster and Megaupload's businesses were shut down by lawsuits, while the owner of Megaupload, Kim Dotcom, was violently arrested during a raid of his home in New Zealand, had his assets seized, and was extradited to the U.S. to face charges. Yet, while predictions were that Internet piracy would increase, over the past few years we've heard fewer and fewer outbursts from these production companies.

As it turns out, the total amount of illegal downloading has been steadily decreasing for the past few years. In particular, the use of torrents to illegally share files has been decreasing drastically. Torrents operate as a peer-to-peer file distribution system and are one of the preferred ways for pirates to illegally copy copyrighted materials due to how easy it is to use them and how secretly people can download illegal copies with them. So what caused illegal downloads to decrease?

The most popular theory is that when primary distributors make their copyrighted work as easily accessible as pirated material, people will switch back to acquiring the work through legal channels. In other words, companies have begun to embrace the convenience of the digital marketplace and are offering safer and faster services than pirates could provide, which has drawn people away from acquiring the work illegally. Pirating always contains a few risks that these services avoid. First, there is always a risk when pirating that a pirate might be caught and sued.

Second, when pirating there is no guarantee that the product downloaded is what it says it is. Oftentimes, individuals will maliciously disguise malware as songs or movies and place it on pirating sites.

New legal distribution systems avoid these risks while being faster (usually) than their illegal counterparts.

In particular, subscription streaming services such as Netflix and Spotify have provided incredibly convenient access to television shows and films, and music, respectively, and have single-handedly had a notable effect on illegal downloads of videos and songs. That is not to say that Internet piracy has gone away. First, just because streaming services are available, doesn't mean that product will not be pirated. For some consumers, even a minimal payment is too much. Second, certain types of products are difficult or impossible to stream, such as computer software, books, and video games. These products will often rely on different types of digital rights management (DRM) software to protect the goods from copying. This software is sometimes a double-edged sword and can encourage potential customers to turn to piracy. This is particularly apparent with video games. Games running with DRM can experience extreme technical issues or can be completely unplayable, while a pirated copy will have the DRM removed and will run without complications, creating a situation where the only people who can play the game properly are pirates. What's more, pirates have begun to compete with streaming sites by streaming content themselves. These sites illegally host streams of television shows or movies for anyone to watch. This causes new problems for companies going after end users of these sites as they never actually download anything on their computer.

The sites themselves are near impossible to completely take down. Some people even illegally stream on popular sites, like Facebook and YouTube. These sites have methods of taking down illegal content, but it is nearly impossible for them to monitor everything that's uploaded to them and remove all uploaded illegal content.

Internet piracy will never go away. Some people will always pirate movies, songs, games, and software. The only question is how to combat this theft. Right now, it looks like the best method is to improve service to the customer and emulate the success that services like Spotify and Netflix have had in regards to reducing Internet piracy. Most people just want to get their entertainment as easily and as quickly as possible. Certainly some products cannot be streamed like books or conventional video games (though that might change in the future), but they can still be offered on services that are easy to use and access like Amazon. So long as piracy is the fastest and easiest way, people will pirate. But, if procuring entertainment becomes easier through legal means rather than illegal ones, then, hopefully, the piracy problem will be minimized.[37]

The last sentence says it all. The intersection between piracy and legal music consumption is ease of use. As a platform, the reason why YouTube has fared so well is because it's extremely easy to use and navigate. In this kind of environment, very few people care to illegally pirate the music if it's all right there and easily accessed for free. You don't even need to physically own any music anymore. Another major issue is the lack of knowledge.

[37] Nevola, J. (2017, November 14). Internet Piracy: The Effects of Streaming Services and the Digital Marketplace. Columbia Science and Technology Law Review. Web: https://tinyurl.com/y72bm7dl

After West End sold, I kept receiving phone calls from fellow creatives, other label owners and artists asking me music business-related questions. *Can you take a look at my royalty statement? I don't understand why I haven't gotten any money. I split from my producing partner and want to go solo. Can you help? Who owns the rights to my music? Why are new versions of my songs being released without my permission?* My buddy Eddie Nicholas is my music co-writer and a longtime collaborator. We spend hours talking about music, music events, music business news, how artists like us make money or don't and why, etc. He, too, would be asked all kinds of questions. He has been releasing music since the 90s and remains a fixture in the house music community. Eddie consults with other creatives, hosts events, writes, records, performs and even caters! By 2014, I was preparing to release my *Freedom* album and Eddie and I began co-writing and releasing a string of songs for other labels. In the days leading up to my album's release, I spent a considerable amount of time sending digital copies to tastemakers and DJs around the world. One was a DJ I met when I played at some house music clubs in Washington, DC in the summer of 1997 while I temp-worked at the World Bank's library department by day. I worked in the basement of this huge office building, compiling and re-shelving library documents. The area around 21st and K Street was always bright and busy. There seemed to be clear and sunny days occurring for weeks at a time in those days. During my lunch break, I'd often walk to the local record store, Twelve Inch Dance, and browse their vinyl stacks. Anyway, this DJ (Taha) was originally from the Sudan. The Sudan is in northern Africa with a coastline on the Red Sea. Sudan shares borders with Egypt, Eritrea, Ethiopia, South Sudan, the Central African Republic, Chad, and

Libya. After years of living in the DC and Virginia area, Taha and his family moved back where he bought a broadcasting signal and launched Capital Radio 91.6 FM.

During the promotions for the *Freedom* album, Taha was kind enough to play the album, in its entirety, live on the air. In talking with him about his station, I asked about any possible openings and a broadcasting partnership began. In the fall of 2014, Eddie and I premiered the *Freedom Radio Hour*, a weekly radio program that combined a DJ mix show with a talk segment, discussing music business news. Eddie and I would discuss the latest news and breakdown the details. I loved how we were able to explain things in a clear and simple manner. Each episode was recorded as an audio podcast and a YouTube video. In what seems like no time, we started to get noticed by some of the biggest names in house music who responded with many positive comments. Through the show, we hoped to help others answer the questions we kept hearing. There was more than altruism at play though. Because the *Freedom Radio Hour* was also a DJ mix show, I would mix in some of the latest Eddie Nicholas, Mixtape Sessions and Honeycomb releases within each episode as another way to promote them. So, the music business news show meant that you were also getting exposed to new music from my associates and me. As the New Year approached, 2015 would become the year that we'd be introduced to another kind of altruism in the form of a streaming music service named TIDAL.

As all of this was happening, I again prepared to send the next round of royalty statements to our artists and pay them.

Chapter 7: Altruism on its Ass

Altruism is the belief in or the practice of selfless concern for the well-being of others and in the spring of 2015, rapper and mogul Jay Z flexed his altruistic muscle while standing on stage in New York City alongside music's mega stars. Usher, Rihanna, Nicki Minaj, Madonna, Deadmau5, Kanye West, Jason Aldean, Jack White, Daft Punk, Beyoncé, Win Butler and others attended the TIDAL launch event at Skylight at Moynihan Station on March 30th. The statement he and these like-minded artists were making was huge. They were taking back control of their art by accepting a higher royalty rate and owning a piece of a streaming company. In TIDAL, Jay Z attempted to not only engage in the streaming wars battle, but he also tried to redefine the landscape for art, artists, royalties and ownership. To be clear again: TIDAL and other streaming outfits pay royalties to labels and music publishers for the permission to offer their music, but Jay Z's statement on stage that night in NYC was a way of putting his competition on notice: we will win at streaming.

Admittedly, his approach was impressive and unlike anything the industry had witnessed. To boot, he had the proverbial backing of the legendary artist, Prince. In TIDAL, Prince found a digital kindred spirit and given Prince's reputation for fighting record labels and challenging distribution norms, the entire industry took notice. Jay Z purchased TIDAL and another company (WiMP) from a Swedish company named Aspiro. The deal was valued at a reported $56 million and included 540,000 subscribers.[38] While Apple Music used the music to sell phones and other devices, TIDAL used high fidelity as a sales gimmick. Here were your choices: you could sign up for TIDAL for $9.99 a month, the quasi-standard price for streaming, or you could opt to pay for 'better quality' streaming at $19.99 a month. The business model always fascinated me. Here was a company that was promising to pay higher royalty rates to its artists, offering a stake in owning the company, but yet, there wasn't a physical product paired with the streaming service, not a phone nor a gadget that coincided with streaming. It was touting high quality streaming and exclusivity. I couldn't understand how their powers-that-be had settled on high fidelity streaming as the gimmick.

Apple was selling iPhones for hundreds of dollars apiece and TIDAL couldn't come up with anything better than an upsell of $10 a month in the form of a Bose-like streaming experience? Bose made its fortune by offering high fidelity speaker systems, but in terms of listening to streamed music, who really cares? For the most part, we are all enjoying music and videos from our devices or computers with crappy speakers. Earbuds are the new speaker systems in the digital marketplace, so why someone would opt to pay for supposed improved quality always perplexed me. I just didn't think that audio quality nor their preponderance towards exclusivity were sustainable models. In a sense, TIDAL wants its customers to suspend disbelief when you consider their exclusivity offer. Jay Z was smart to leverage his position as president of Def Jam Recordings to

---

[38] Snider, M. (2016, March 31). Jay Z sues previous owners of music service TIDAL. USA Today. Web: https://tinyurl.com/yc5ntsg2

regain control of his masters. When he bragged that Rihanna, Kanye West and all of their music would be available on the TIDAL service only, it seemed like a great way to control their copyright, but as always, technology has a way of reminding us how much faster it runs than the rest of its counterparts. TIDAL isn't the only service to fall prey to a false sense of exclusivity. On the surface it makes sense. *Sign up with us and you'll get access to these artists only. They aren't available on any other platform but ours.* But when technology enters the space, it says, *No, we'll easily find a way to rip or steal that music or content and offer it up in a pirated manner.*

On top of all of this, their main competitor (free music on YouTube) continued to thrive. By the time TIDAL came to the U.S., the streaming wars were nearing a fever pitch. Apple, who had always paired media with a product, was eager to launch their own subscription service. Up until its official announcement on June 30, 2015, Apple had built quite a digital media empire within its Apple Music department. On June 7, 2015, Sony Music CEO Doug Morris confirmed that Apple had plans to announce a music streaming service and that it had $178 billion dollars in the bank and 800 million credit cards in iTunes.[39] Apple put its best foot forward and provided a solid fiscal foundation from which to build a streaming subscription service. Apple Music launched that summer in 2015 and within two years, built a subscription base currently north of 30 million paid subscribers. Apple also changed the game in terms of pairing products with services, making it nearly impossible for anyone else, TIDAL especially, to

---

[39] Heisler, Y. (2015, June 25). Revealed: How Much Apple is Paying Artists on Apple Music (it's Less Than You Might Think). Web: https://bgr.com/2015/06/25/apple-music-royalty-payments-2/

build a robust and sustainable streaming service without that pairing component in place. In contrast to Apple, TIDAL seemed to be leveraging artist brands with exclusive streaming and high fidelity, but not with a physical product. Part of the streaming wars fight isn't just to get a customer to commit to paying $10 a month for unlimited streaming. It's also a fight for exclusive content. Each of the popular services today pitch exclusivity to its customers. A Taylor Swift fan? You can only get her music there. A Kanye West fan? Oh, you can only get his music here. But after watching Apple Music and TIDAL battle it out for exclusive album releases over the past year, and attracting just over 20 million subscribers between them, some major record label executives began to argue that limiting new releases to one service—even for a week or two—could be costing them, despite the support they get for the exclusive deals. They worry that limiting an album's availability during its busiest period reduces listening and frustrates subscribers of services that don't have the album. "All the exclusives feel erratic at the moment," said Steve Cooper, chief executive of Access Industries' Warner Music Group in a recent interview with *Music Business Worldwide*, an online publication. "That's confusing to fans, and that's not good for the industry."[40] Cooper's comments seem to cement the argument that exclusivity is no longer a profit motive for these streaming organizations. I enjoyed the attribution of 'confusion' given to customers, but the truth is, exclusivity was a gamble with no sustainable plan from any of these services. Simply put: exclusivity didn't make them enough money to sustain that business model.

---

[40] Karp, H. (2016, September 8). Music Industry Hits Pause on Exclusive Album-Release Deals. Wall Street Journal. Web: https://tinyurl.com/yady62mt

In the case of TIDAL, once you remove exclusivity, what's left is a failing and unsustainable sales model.

Then, a funny thing happened in May of 2015 when a music industry bomb exploded that barely got any real press or notice, but spoke volumes about the way the biggest record labels in the world were profiting from Spotify, while perhaps circumventing their breakage policy. I'll explain. Up until this point, artists are privy to very few details related to deals between labels and distributors, both physical and digital. In the case of streaming services like Spotify, transparency just isn't there. These deals are private-- plain and simple-- but in May of 2011, a contract between Sony, one of the three biggest labels, and Spotify was leaked.

> In it, Spotify agreed to pay advances of US $42.5 million to Sony Music in three years. Exhibit 4(a) of the contract stipulates advance payments of US $9 million for the first year, US $16 million for the second year and US $17.5 million for an optional third year.

> Breakage is an advance payment from a streaming service to a record label that exceeds royalty payments in a given period. The record labels are criticized for not sharing this "breakage" money with the artists. All three major companies rejected the accusations and argued that they share advances with the artists. A spokesman of Warner Music Group is cited in *Music Business Worldwide* with saying: "Warner Music shares all advances, minimum guarantees and 'flat fees' with its artists. This policy has been in effect at Warner Music since 2009,

purposely treating breakage like other digital revenue." In the same article, a Sony statement is cited where the company says it shares money from breakage and advances with its artists: Sony Music historically has shared digital breakage with its artists, and voluntarily credits breakage from all digital services to artist accounts.

Under the Sony Music 'Breakage Policy,' SME shares with its recording artists all unallocated income from advances, non-recoupable payments and minimum revenue guarantees that Sony Music receives under its digital distribution deals. This applies to all revenue under digital catalogue distribution agreements, whether or not the guarantees, advances or 'flat' payments can be associated with individual master transactions." A few days after the article was published, a Universal Music Group spokesman confirmed that the company shares "with artists' minimum guarantees as well as unrecouped digital advances, where they exist." However, in a Billboard Magazine guest post, Darius Van Arman, who serves on the boards of the indie trade body A2IM, digital collecting society SoundExchange and indie licensing agency MERLIN critically commented on the majors' 'breakage' policy: "Whereas the majors typically share breakage only when required to do so in their contracts with big artists or larger distributed labels (except for Warner Music Group, who has a more progressive stance and who sometimes volunteers to share breakage)."

The authors of the *Rethink Music* report also question the assurances of the major labels and state: "Our analysis of Universal's accounting statements show no evidence of the payment of breakage to artists" (Rethink Music, 2015: 16). However, the pros and cons highlight that there is still a need to bring more transparency into the business practices surrounding music streaming. So, do they pay their artists as stipulated by their respective breakage policies or don't they? And if they do, do they pay out a commensurate rate based on income?

Without any real transparency, we'll never know. Furthermore, if this contract had never been leaked, we'd still be trying to connect the dots between label and publisher income vs. artist income. Again, transparency in this regard just isn't there. A side note worth noting here: Labels will have artists think that rampant piracy is to blame for profit losses, but news of the leaked Sony-Spotify deal put to bed any doubts.

The truth is that a tremendous amount of money is being made by these major labels, but when it comes to royalty bearing income, the mystery around income sources, units sold and stream counts persists.

The leaked deal didn't just spell out the details between Sony and Spotify as it relates to streaming Sony's content on the streaming platform. It also leaked details around advertising space on the service. In addition to the advance Spotify must pay Sony Music, it is also required to give the music label free ad space on its service.

The "credit for advertising inventory" clause mentioned in section 14(a) grants Sony Music a total of $9 million in ad space ($2.5 million in the first year, and $3 million and $3.5 million in the subsequent years). And the free ads don't come at market rates either — they must be given to Sony Music at a heavily discounted rate.[41]

The caveat in the deal is that Sony Music can spend these dollars however it chooses. In other words, if they decide to sub contract this ad space and create a side business, they can sell it on as they wish, which arguably circumvents the breakage policy.

If, for instance, Sony Music decides to sell ad space on the Spotify platform to Comcast, do the artists in Sony Music's roster benefit as well or just the corporation? How can we check? Oh right... we can't.

---

[41] Singleton, M. (2015, May 19). This was Sony Music's contract with Spotify. The Verge. Web: https://www.theverge.com/2015/5/19/8621581/sony-music-spotify-contract

Chapter 8: Exclusivity and the Superfans That Don't Care

Piracy in the age of streaming is a strange thing. On the surface, it gives the world a false sense. Some industry insiders will have you believe that streaming not only saved the music industry, but it also severely curtailed piracy because why would you pirate content that you can access for free on YouTube and the like? Streaming, in part, was put on a pedestal because of the false sense that it had marginalized online piracy, but the truth is that piracy persists even in the era of streaming:

> But, with the advent of the Internet, torrenting had become commonplace with listeners favoring illegal downloads over paying for music. However, the rise in streaming has been hailed by some as a potential saving grace for the music industry. A 2015 study by the European Commission showed a decrease in piracy as a result of the easy access to streaming services. But with the recent influx of albums exclusive to one service, reports once again show high piracy rates for albums released as exclusives. Following TIDAL's exclusive release of Kanye West's *The Life of Pablo* on Saturday, February 13, 2016, the album amassed over 500,000 illegal downloads by Tuesday, just three days later, according to TorrentFreak.

Another high piracy count came just six months later when Frank Ocean released his sophomore album, *Blonde*, exclusively through iTunes and Apple Music. According to *Music Business Worldwide*, citing data provided by "content protection, market tracking and audience connection solutions" specialist MUSO, *Blonde* had been illegally downloaded over 750,000 times in less than a week following its August 20, 2016 release. While the album was released to other services at later times, MUSO shows over 2.3 million illegal downloads as of October 6, 2016. These increases in piracy are perceived to stem from the lack of availability of certain albums across streaming platforms.[42]

So, what are torrents?

Torrents are simply 'files' that hold information related to other files and folders that are to be distributed. When you download a movie or music torrent, for example, this 'torrent file' contains necessary information which will let you download that movie or song.

When you start downloading the files associated with that torrent, you might also see a file that is not familiar with those other chunks of data. Those are values which are used to verify a file.[43]

[42] Dziawura, C. (2016, November 16). Exclusive Album Releases raise new concerns in Music Industry. Northeast Valley News. Web: https://tinyurl.com/yboryzv3

[43] Fossbytes Staff. (2017, May 1). What Are Torrents? How Torrent Works? — BitTorrenting 101. Fossbytes. Web: https://fossbytes.com/how-torrent-works-what-is-bittorrenting/

To me, torrents work much like the *AOL Instant Messengers*, *Napsters* and *Kazaas* of yesteryear. It uses peer-to-peer technology to share and exchange files and folders. Any way you look at it, its original intent was to share media without first paying the creators of that media. Why else would the RIAA want to wage such a fight against The Pirate Bay, for example? That was a Google-like search engine that centralized access to these torrents.

Stream-ripping, torrenting and illegal downloading mean that piracy is still here and has adapted with the digital times. People will access music irrespective of whether it's paid for or not. These particular issues notwithstanding, 2016 turned out to be an extremely eye-awakening year in a completely unexpected way. To begin with, you couldn't escape the streaming oligarchy that took hold by 2016. By this point, you'd be hard-pressed to quickly name any other streaming service outside of the six biggest: Amazon, Apple Music, Pandora, Spotify, TIDAL, and YouTube. Article after article touted the music 'salvation' that streaming had become to many, but the math never seemed to add up. If so much of the world has been streaming music, why are the artists ending up with so little, a fraction of a penny per stream, in fact? Back at TIDAL headquarters, the math didn't seem to be adding up for Jay Z either. By the spring of 2016, his team filed suit against the previous owners of TIDAL with claims that they were given inflated subscriber numbers.

> The legal action was first reported by Norwegian press as a "giant lawsuit" seeking $15 million from Scandinavian company Aspiro and major shareholders. Jay Z launched TIDAL in the U.S. one year ago after paying Aspiro $56 million.

"It became clear after taking control of TIDAL and conducting our own audit that the total number of subscribers was actually well below the 540,000 reported to us by the prior owners," the company said in a statement sent to *USA TODAY*. "As a result, we have now served legal notice to parties involved in the sale. While we cannot share further comment during active legal proceedings, we're proud of our success and remain focused on delivering the best experience for artists and fans."[44]

Digital music came in and instantly touted two things that were underappreciated by the industry. Digital music was easy to use. You didn't have to leave your house to buy and download music. So, ease of use was a big selling point to consumers. The other was a complete abandonment of the physical good. Buying and downloading meant your storage needs were completely different and gone were the days of making shelf space in your living room for CDs or vinyl when you could now store hundreds of albums on your computer. No fuss. No muss. Fast-forward a short amount of time and we're now in a culture where you don't even need offline storage to manage your music collection. Your music collection sits on the Internet somewhere, out of your way, ready for you to access whenever you wish. Think: ease of use times one million! So, now you don't have the experience of holding that special package I was mentioning earlier.

[44] Snider, M. (2016, March 31). Jay Z sues previous owners of music service TIDAL. USA Today. Web:
https://www.usatoday.com/story/tech/news/2016/03/31/jay-z-sues-previous-owners-music-service-tidal/82460988/

You can't hold the package and read through the liner notes and enjoy those custom made photographs, made *exclusively* for you, the person who bought it. Now, it all sits somewhere, invisible. There's nothing of substance in the music consumption experience to physically connect you with the artists you fall in love with.

Anybody who knows me knows that I'm a big Janet Jackson fan. Since I was a kid, I remember becoming spellbound by how beautifully different she was. What she was singing about spoke to me (ahem. . . CONTROL . . . what kid didn't want more of that?) and how she presented herself resonated. She was her brother's sister for sure, but Janet to me was also uniquely different. She even danced and moved differently. I poured over every album like it was a book, engulfed every song and every music video with my eyes and heart, and connected my love for music with her love of being amazing and poof! We were kindred spirits. Ok ok. I know I'm going a little bit overboard, but my point in bringing all of this up is to point out that the consumer made the kind of connection that was so deep and so profound that it acted like a glue that stuck to that artist for decades, if not forever. Digital music and then streaming music completely tore away at the fabric of that kind of connection. Today, we're experiencing the digital streaming medium where packaging is so yesterday. Albums are bits you pick at in order to curate the best mega album you've ever heard. This super album isn't by one artist; it's comprised of many artists from across different genres. While a traditional album is roughly forty-five minutes in total length, a playlist can last all day long and can run for several hours at a time.

Once you click on the 'loop' or 'shuffle' buttons, your playlist will live in the background, throughout the day as you attend to your daily tasks. The playlist, in this context, is king and you're the head of A&R for your own virtual label. In a sense, you need the artist to feed you content, but you don't need to invest in the artist enough where a glue develops between fan and artist. Let's be clear about what this means. What technology companies have done is shift consumer behaviors by completely conditioning us into adopting a new way of listening to music. Record companies in the early digital music days completely overlooked the tear in the value system that Apple created and that they co-signed. This, to me, speaks to how far behind record companies have always been in terms of technological advances. By late 2015, articles began to surface about the impact of music in the era of the *superfan* after media and technology analysis firm MIDiA Research released an infographic on streaming users' listening habits. There's also a distinction between an *artist superfan* and a *streaming superfan* that's worth noting.

In *Forbes*, author Cherie Hu, wrote:

> The prominence of streaming services is leading to the emergence of a new dichotomy of superfandom in music—the artist superfan versus the streaming superfan (a.k.a. the paying streaming subscriber). A standard framework for understanding the artist superfan is laid out in the film *Super Fans: The Future of the Music Industry*.

Co-produced by direct-to-fan music platform PledgeMusic and online education company Lynda.com, the video defines superfans as those who are willing to pay the most to connect on a deeper level with artists, and provides action items for artists to maximize their superfans' engagement.

First, artists themselves need to work toward increasing their own exposure, "one fan at a time," instead of relying on labels to do the job. Second, artists need to foster bidirectional conversation with their listeners and foster a personal relationship that extends beyond music.

The MIDiA findings show that a crucial difference between the artist superfan and the streaming superfan is the extent of engagement and conversation. As subscribers actively discover new music and spend less time with each individual album, their tastes are characterized by greater breadth at the expense of depth. They seem to consume music like the average Internet user consumes news: as brief sound bites that expire within an increasingly short period of time before being engulfed by new content.

In fact, this more transient behavior could be generalized to all music consumers, not just paying subscribers. "We are now living in the attention economy, where people make investments in artists with their time, not necessarily with cold hard cash," explains MIDiA founder Mark Mulligan.

"Hence we see an increasing amount of competition for time—if you're streaming an artist or album for free, it's only one of a whole bunch of albums that are being pushed to you that same day or week.

People inherently develop shallower relationships with artists in such an environment."[45]

I argue that it is the digital music landscape itself that is shallow in terms of fostering that fan-to-artist connection, which then perpetuates a culture where people develop shallower relationships all around.

Jay Z's journey with creating a platform in TIDAL proved arduous by 2016 and with more reports about streaming music to come, his sense of altruism would be tested, since after all, this business, despite how shallow the relationship, is made up of people who engage in an interplay between art, business and corporatism.

---

[45] Hu, C. (2015, November 10). How Music Streaming Is Creating A New Type Of Superfan. Forbes. Web: https://www.forbes.com/sites/cheriehu/2015/11/10/how-music-streaming-is-creating-a-new-type-of-superfan/#701d9ed931d6

Chapter 9: Fake News and Album Fumbles

Success in the age of streaming is also a strange thing. In streaming, subscriber numbers and stream counts have replaced the traditional 1:1 sales structure that long dominated the industry. Until streaming, the music business relied on Nielsen reports to know how the sales of a record fared.

> Nielsen is the authority in tracking what music people are buying both in-store and digitally. Nielsen compiles data from more than 39,000 retail outlets globally, to help record labels, publishers, artists, artist management, and performance rights organizations understand which albums, singles and music videos people are buying, and where they're buying them. On a weekly basis, Nielsen collects point-of-sale (POS) data in 19 countries. In the U.S. and Canada, physical and digital titles from venues, mass merchants, retail chains, independent record stores and digital download providers can be viewed via tracking systems such as UPC (Universal Product Code) and ISRC (International Standard Recording Code) as well as artist, market, retailer type or genre.[46]

---

[46] Nielson Staff. (2018). Music Sales Measurement. Nielson. Web: http://www.nielsen.com/us/en/solutions/measurement/music-sales-measurement.html

Every time the sales person swiped your vinyl, cassette tape or CD selection across a reader and you heard that infamous beep sound, you knew that there was data being transmitted to someone or something as it recorded the sales transaction. For the industry, it was a much simpler time in terms of the mathematics. For a long time, the consensus was that each sale of music was thought of as one unit sold. Simple, right? 500,000 units sold meant that your record went "gold." 1,000,000 units sold meant that your record went "platinum." Since the dawn of music sales measurement, we long-valued this sales system, pushing and promoting terms like "double platinum," "triple platinum," and "diamond" into our popular music lexicon. The moment that Apple secured licensing deals with the biggest record labels at the beginning of the digital music revolution, the value system around 'units sold' completely changed. A purchased vinyl, cassette tape or CD is considered 1 unit sold. After Apple's installation of their 99¢ per download model, now each individual song could be purchased. The sales transaction was no longer dependent on the consumer being forced to download an entire album if they were only interested in one or two songs. Apple's download model caused a dramatic shift. It completely devalued the full length album which was long held as the anchor to a recording artist's creative expression. The album was the culmination of creative ideas-- a journey, a diving into the artist's mind. From the LP or "long play," you got to understand and appreciate the true essence of your favorite artists. You might sit through some of the songs that are less favorable to you because the exercise was to take in the full album. This is where the connection from fan to artist proved vital.

Before social media, the album and the album's physical packaging provided that deep connection with an artist. You could read their words, learn who they worked with and enjoy photographs exclusively produced for that album. There's that word again . . . *exclusive*. The value of one unit sold made total sense in this paradigm. You were buying access to a club of other fans who enjoyed this exclusive experience that only happened once you bought the album. The better or the more popular the album, the more you wanted to physically own, not just the music, but the package it came in as well. For the consumer, streaming music means accepting unlimited access over ownership, but as a record label, music publisher, or say, Billboard music, it means accepting that unit values can be manipulated in more ways than ever before. However, if you paid attention to the strategy around singer Prince's 2004 *Musicology* album release, we saw a shift in this value system coming. In support of his tour, every person who purchased a ticket to the *Musicology* tour received a "complimentary" copy of the album. At the time, MTV.com had this to report:

> Discussions about the novel approach to selling records began when *Musicology* was released April 20th. Tickets sold for concerts taking place prior to the release of the album didn't count toward the album's total, since a pre-existing policy dictates that Billboard doesn't recognize albums sold in an "exclusive window," such as Internet presales, but after April 20, all tickets sold for the handful of shows Prince had scheduled in a given week, each with attendance around 10,000, counted toward his album-sales total.

And with around three or four shows scheduled per week through September 9, *Musicology* doesn't look like it'll be disappearing from the chart anytime soon.

Billboard chart editor Geoff Mayfield claims that 25 percent, or 158,000 copies, of *Musicology's* total sales were through concert tickets, priced at $75-$85.

While Prince's initiative may seem like a good way to introduce fans of *Purple Rain*, *1999* or *Diamonds and Pearls* to his new material, it may put unwanted multiple copies in the hands of his followers. For instance, if a married couple attended a show, they'd come home with two copies in hand. Should they attend multiple shows, even more copies would clutter their CD collection.

And should these Prince fans be completists, they may prefer having the CD packaged in a jewel case with the complete artwork, instead of the cardboard sleeves the concert copies come in — warranting yet another copy brought home. Protected by a grandfather clause, *Musicology* will be allowed to continue counting albums sold through concert tickets toward its total, since Mayfield said it would be unfair to "change horses in the middle of the stream," but other artists who may have been eyeing Prince's strategy might be impeded.[47]

---

[47] DeAngelo, J. (2004, May 28). Billboard Sours on Prince's Musicology Sales Experiment. MTV. Web:
http://www.mtv.com/news/1488027/billboard-sours-on-princes-musicology-sales-experiment/

Always the consummate musician's musician, Prince seemed to regularly challenge belief systems around music and music's value. In 2007, he applied the same sales gimmick using a different UK paper with the release of his *Planet Earth* CD. At the time, *The Mail* had this to say:

> In an unprecedented deal, Prince granted British tabloid *The Mail* exclusive rights to distribute his album as a freebie. Cutting out record stores, online sellers, and even his UK label at the time, Sony BMG, he decided to take *Planet Earth* straight to the people, and all it cost them was the paper's $3 cover price. "It's direct marketing," the pint-sized popstar said when the deal was announced. "And I don't have to be in the speculation business of the record industry, which is going through a lot of tumultuous times right now."
>
> As his fans rejoice — another middle finger to The Man! — the music industry is reeling. While *Planet Earth* was due to hit shelves in the U.S. on July 24, 2007, Sony BMG announced that with so many free copies floating around, it wouldn't release the album for sale in the UK at all. Music retailers boycotted the paper, until HMV reluctantly agreed to stock it, just this once. "We decided we could either get marginalized or we could get right in there," says spokesman Gennaro Castaldo. "With whatever reservations, our motivation was to give our customers the choice and access to the album."[48]

---

[48] Farouky, J. (2007, July 18). Why Prince's Free CD Ploy Worked. Time. Web: http://content.time.com/time/arts/article/0,8599,1644427,00.html

Because of the challenges Prince posed by virtue of these actions, other artists began to conceive of other inventive ways to deliver their music to fans in unprecedented ways. Taking his cue from Prince and other such visionaries, Jay Z experimented with album distribution himself. In 2013 and as part of a broader deal between Samsung and Roc Nation - estimated at $20 million - a total of one million copies of Jay Z's album, *Magna Carta Holy Grail*, were given away at one minute past midnight, a full 72 hours before it officially went on sale. Samsung, a Korea based mobile company, paid $5 million so that the first million owners of Galaxy S III, Galaxy S4 and Galaxy Note II devices were able to claim the album through a free app from the Google Play store.

In the self-referential bubble of the music business, much has been made of the fact that, because it is free to consumers, those 1 million "sales" did not count towards the charts in the US, the UK and elsewhere because of chart rules.

But at $5 a copy, Jay Z is almost certainly getting a far higher royalty rate than he would if those sales came from download stores or the dwindling number of record shops. The album is already a banker in an age when there are, in sales terms, few superstar certainties.

The scale of the deal did, however, force the RIAA to make significant tweaks to its gold and platinum awards program, meaning Jay Z received his platinum sales plaque at the time of the release rather than having to wait 30 days (as per the old sales certification rules).

This covered any digital album sales that previously had to wait a month to be qualified in order to allow for "returns" (unsold, but shipped, stock) - a throwback to the days when music was only available on physical formats. Yet within this all is a burning contradiction. The one million album downloads are disqualified from the chart for being "free" to the consumer, but they count towards that RIAA sales plaque because someone (in this case, Samsung) paid for them.[49]

That following year, Billboard's value system around total sales would be tested yet again with legendary rock band U2. In 2014, the band released their 13th studio album, *Songs of Innocence*, in collaboration with Apple Music. At midnight on September 9th, Apple's 500 million subscribers discovered that a copy of the new album was sitting in their library, available to download for free. According to front man Bono, the reason for offering the album for free was to promote their upcoming *Songs of Innocence* Global Tour. Coming off for their previous, overly expensive "360" tour, U2 had seats to fill and costs to keep down. Now, on the surface you might think that this might be an excellent marketing idea. Give 500 million people access to a legendary band's latest album for nothing. What could go wrong? Well, for starters, distributing content to users who never gave consent is always problematic. In U2's case, the album felt forced upon the consumer, like a virus installed onto your system overnight.

---

[49] Forde, E. (2013, July 4). Jay-Z's Samsung deal signals a musical future where the rich get richer. The Guardian. Web: https://www.theguardian.com/music/musicblog/2013/jul/04/jay-z-samsung-music-future

Receiving an album you never asked for felt violating. Beyond this, there were practical problems that Apple and U2 underappreciated. At more than 48 minutes long, U2's 11-song album took up quite a bit of space in your iTunes library and if you were on your last bits of space on your phone or computer, you were forced to delete files in order to sync your phone or backup your device. It was rude and a pain in the ass to get rid of. Rumors began to swirl that Apple sent the album in such a way as to make it impossible to ever fully delete it. Allegedly, because it was "free," users couldn't opt out. This reminded me of the old Windows operating system that forced users to use the Internet Explorer browser. Once Mozilla's Firefox, Google Chrome and Safari began to outshine Internet Explorer and users attempted to uninstall the default browser, it remained installed in the background. Because of whatever deal was struck, the users paid the price by having to deal with an operating system that forced a free product on them. Sound familiar?

Marco Arment, a former executive at Tumblr and a technology developer, said: "The damage here isn't that a bunch of people need to figure out how to delete an album that they got for free and are now whining about it. It's that Apple did something inconsiderate, tone-deaf, and kinda creepy for the sake of a relatively unimportant marketing campaign, and they seemingly didn't think it would be a problem."[50]

---

[50] Sherwin, A. (2014, September 19). Free U2 album: How the most generous giveaway in music history turned PR disaster. Independent. Web: https://www.independent.co.uk/arts-entertainment/music/features/free-u2-album-how-the-most-generous-giveaway-in-music-history-turned-into-a-pr-disaster-9745028.html

CEO Tim Cook had Apple issue a statement of apology as well as instructions for deleting the album from your iTunes library. To boot, *Songs of Innocence* was not eligible to chart on Billboard until it was commercially released on October 14, 2014, a full month after *free-download-gate*. In its first tracking week of sales, it sold 28,000 copies, and debuted and peaked at No. 9 on the Billboard 200.[51] Adding to the reported $52 million that Apple paid UMG's Interscope Records for the rights made this quite a P.R. disaster!

There are a few layers to dissect from the U2 story, but much of it went unreported. For instance, *Songs of Innocence* managed to peak at No. 9 on the Billboard 200, but with 28,000 copies sold in its first week, one had to notice and ponder some valid questions. Did a sudden sales surge occur after the first week or was there funny math at work? And with none of the pre-release activity counted towards positioning within the Billboard charts, then perhaps Marco Arment had a point in asking the right question. Why was Apple Music willing to engage in such a foolish and unimportant exercise for a slew of free downloads that cost them millions? Did the means justify the ends? Let's take a look at some real math. As of 2018 and just four years after the U2 debacle, Apple Music is worth a reported $10 billion with 36 million paid subscribers signed up for the service.[52]

---

[51] Caulfield, K. (2017, December 5). U2's 'Songs of Experience' Heading for No. 1 on Billboard 200 Albums Chart. Billboard. Web: https://www.billboard.com/articles/columns/chart-beat/8061700/u2-songs-of-experience-heading-no-1-billboard-200

[52] Duggan, W. (2018, February 28). Apple Music Is Now Worth $10 Billion. U.S News & World Report. Web: https://money.usnews.com/investing/stock-market-news/articles/2018-02-28/apple-inc-aapl-stock

Consider the iPhone and you'll realize that this is where Apple is really winning. Thanks to their iPhone products and the music they include, Apple is now worth a staggering $1 trillion!

Apple gambled with music and was rewarded handsomely for it. As a tech giant, they remained at the forefront of what customers wanted and never wavered in their determination. From the 99¢-per-download strategy to their efforts to pair music with a mobile product, Apple used 'ease of use' and 'access over ownership' to deliver music and other media before the music business could. Now, let's consider U2 in this scenario. Let us remember that a tour in support of the album was going to evaporate any losses from their previous, yet hugely expensive "360" tour. In support of *Songs of Innocence,* how did U2 fare with their 2015 "Innocence + Experience" tour? According to Billboard, the North American leg of their 36 shows grossed $76,166,563 from 650,582 tickets sold; all shows were sold-out. In total, the tour grossed $152.2 million from 1,286,416 tickets sold, making U2 the fourth-highest-grossing artist of 2015.[53] I'll call this a fraction of a trillion!

So, the experiment worked. When you're of the caliber of U2, Jay Z Prince and Beyoncé, it pays to innovate. They've each co-opted technology with media to challenge the status quo. How much attention can you attract when you surprise-release your album with no advance marketing? How many tickets do you sell when you pair them with the purchase of a newspaper? How many albums get sold

[53] Waddell, R. (2015, August 4). U2 Closes N. American Leg of Innocence + Experience With 150,000 New York Fans. Billboard. Web: https://www.billboard.com/articles/business/6655667/u2-bruce-springsteen-north-american-innocence-experience-76-million

when you pair it with the release of a new smartphone? How profitable does your tour become if you give away a new album for free with every ticket purchase?

The glaring omission in this fabulous utopia is the independent artist. If you're the 1%, these experiments work. But what about the rest—the 99% of recording artists who aren't U2, Prince or Beyoncé, but are earning a fraction of a penny per stream from their music? Where's their fiscal boost? Simply put: without touring (i.e. pairing), substantial income just isn't there.

As all of this was happening, I again prepared to send the next round of royalty statements to our artists and pay them.

Chapter 10: Myths, Money and Mergers

TIDAL had quite the year in 2016. As they were gearing up to legally fight Aspiro, the Norwegian company that previously owned TIDAL, Westbury Road and Roc Nation had just released singer Rihanna's eighth studio album, *ANTI*. In true *streaming wars* fashion, TIDAL wanted to tout the success of its exclusive star by applying the Jay Z / Samsung method a la his *Magna Carta Holy Grail*.

> Rihanna's *ANTI* album, which came out after a drawn-out marketing campaign and a last-minute leak, was released with help from a sponsorship deal with Samsung in which one million copies were given away to fans. Those downloads led the RIAA to immediately certify *ANTI* as a platinum release. TIDAL further said that it had sold 484,833 downloads of the album, in addition to those given away as part of the Samsung promotion, and that the album was streamed 5.6 million times on its service.[54]

There has never been a more confusing time to watch the music charts. The 'units sold' model has been completely reimagined, warping how we view success in terms of hit songs.

---

[54] Sisario, B. (2016, February 1). Rihanna's 'Anti' Sells Fewer Than 1,000 Copies in U.S., but Some Call It a Hit. New York Times. Web: https://www.nytimes.com/2016/02/02/arts/music/rihanna-anti-chart-tidal-debut-sales.html?ref=topics

The data that used to support that platinum status recognition is no longer supportive.

> To adapt, Billboard has to fold in radio airplay, traditional sales, digital sales, and streaming data to accurately depict the popularity of new singles and albums; artists are partnering with streaming services and tech companies for promotional campaigns and exclusivity windows; release dates are being thrown into the wind, rendered totally meaningless by the digital era.[55]

Then, there's Frank Ocean.

> The Grammy-winning R&B singer released two albums and a full-color, high-gloss magazine over the course of two days. In doing so, he injected enthusiasm, confusion and yet more chaos into an ever-evolving music business. The unveiling-- the latest in a line of innovative, high-profile maneuvers-- disrupted the US album charts. Where did Ocean end up on the chart? At No. 1, but how he got there is not as simple as it used to be.

> According to Billboard's Top 200 album count, the Apple Music-released *Blonde* debuted at No. 1, with a first-week tally of over 275,000 "equivalent album units" sold—note the wording in quotes.

[55] Cox, J. (2016, February 5). Rihanna, the RIAA, and making a platinum record in 2016. The Verge. Web:
https://www.theverge.com/2016/2/5/10923826/rihanna-anti-platinum-album-riaa-streaming-2016

So, what, exactly, is an "equivalent album?" It's a complicated mashup of streaming and sales data, where 10 digital-track downloads sold and 1,500 songs streamed are equal to one album. In Ocean's case, he sold 232,000 digital-album downloads of *Blonde*, according to Nielsen Music. The album then accrued 65 million streams of its individual tracks. That number in turn is divided by 1,500 to arrive at what, for charting purposes, essentially amounts to an additional 43,000 albums sold (individual tracks from the release were not made for sale).

Got all that? You're forgiven if not.

"It's kind of the Wild West and it always has been. People are just trying to figure it all out," says Tim Smith, who as founder of Blood Company manages major electronic artists including Skrillex, Zedd and Boys Noize. In recent years the task of tabulating a record's success and popularity has grown more complicated. What used to be an album sale is now an "equivalent album sale." Each component—that is, a song—of a release—otherwise known as a project—is measured and weighted using industry-approved equations.

Simple math? Far from it.

Whereas one album plus another album once equaled two albums, in an on-demand era of streaming and instant downloads, one better bring a calculator to unravel the new chart language.

What was once as simple as adding up the sales of a few different formats has now become a Ph.D. worthy calculation. Trying to distill it all are companies like Nielsen Music and BuzzAngle, which track physical and digital sales and streaming data in order to gauge success in an evolving, fluid business.

"When you say it's the top album, you have to clarify that," says Jim Lidestri, CEO of Border City Music, which owns BuzzAngle. "What does that mean?"[56]

By 2017, Billboard announced that that it was retooling the formulation of its charts, which are compiled by Nielsen Music.

"Beginning in 2018, plays occurring on paid subscription-based music services (such as Amazon Music and Apple Music) or on the paid subscription tiers of hybrid paid/ad supported platforms (such as SoundCloud and Spotify) will be given more weight in chart calculations than those plays on pure ad-supported services (such as YouTube) or on the non-paid tiers of hybrid paid/ad-supported services," Billboard said. The statement went on to clarify that video streams would not count into the album chart calculations. Jimmy Iovine, who is head of Apple Music, has been arguing against YouTube growing its influence. He told NBC News that artists say they work with YouTube to promote their records because it currently counts the same as a paid stream.

---

[56] Roberts, R. (2016, August 30). What makes for a No. 1 album in the on-demand age of streaming? LA Times. Web:
http://www.latimes.com/entertainment/music/la-et-ms-music-charts-20160822-snap-story.html

"How can the record industry let that go down? It is not in their interest to promote a free tier." He also described YouTube as "fake news," meaning that its traffic is open to manipulation.[57]

Iovine is correct on that last point. YouTube's traffic *is* open to manipulation. Do a simple Google search for "buying YouTube likes" and you'll come across a myriad of services, like Fiverr for example, that boast freelance servicing. On this site, freelancers offer to increase the amount of likes on your social media pages for $5 (hence, the name). So if Billboard is tabulating its latest hit music charts and is including YouTube stats with equal weight as paid streams or physical units, then what does it mean, mathematically, to have a #1 hit song on the charts today?

In January 2017, TIDAL removed the altruism from their core beliefs. This was the kind of altruism that I talked about earlier—the promise of artists owning a stake in their own streaming service and being paid a higher royalty rate for streamed music. This was the kind of company that was out for a fairer share for art and for artists. All of them, except for TIDAL, were owned by huge tech giants. The truth is, however, that TIDAL had been in a world of trouble for a while. As I mentioned, its value and its subscriber base was in question; it seemed to be more expensive than the others for no good reason and it never paired its services with a physical product that people wanted.

---

[57] Atkinson, C. (2017, October 20). Billboard Magazine Won't Add YouTube Views Into Its Album Charts. NBC News. Web: https://www.nbcnews.com/pop-culture/music/billboard-magazine-won-t-add-youtube-views-its-album-charts-n812331

Almost since Jay Z took it over, the service has been the subject of speculation that it would fail or be purchased by a deep-pocket competitor like Apple.

But Jay Z found a lifeline through a deal in which Sprint bought a one-third stake in the service for an undisclosed amount. The arrangement injected some needed investment in TIDAL and allowed it, at least for now, to remain an underdog in a streaming market that has become dominated by giants. "TIDAL has struggled to make a dent in the streaming market and has shallower pockets than Spotify, Apple or Amazon," said Mark Mulligan, an analyst at MIdia Research. "The Sprint deal gives it access to a big customer base, free marketing and a war chest to take on the streaming incumbents."[58]

TIDAL was the last man standing, so to speak, but it went corporate and without that altruism, streaming, writ large, has become completely corporatized.

Back at Honeycomb Music, we released a string of great projects while Josh Milan continued working on his debut double album release, entitled *6.9.69*, in honor of his birthday. He had been working in secret for the better part of nine years, tinkering and chiseling away at what I think is a masterpiece of an album. A valuable skill set I developed over the years and after some schooling was "mastering." In short, mastering is the final step of audio post-production.

---

[58] Sisario, B. (2017, January 23). TIDAL, Jay Z's Streaming Service, Sells a Stake to Sprint. New York Times. Web: https://www.nytimes.com/2017/01/23/business/media/tidal-streaming-music-jayz-sprint.html?_r=0

The purpose of mastering is to balance sonic elements of a stereo mix and optimize playback across all systems and media formats. Traditionally, mastering is done using tools like equalization, compression, limiting and stereo enhancement. I had been mastering all of Honeycomb's releases after "Your Body," but mastering Josh's solo album was a true honor. To boot, he hired famed mastering guru Dave Darlington to mix and master the 'live band' sections of the double album. This meant that my mastering work was placed alongside a legend in the field. To be honest, I was overwhelmed with a sense of enormous responsibility and humility.

In the name of pairing the release, Josh and I arranged for Honeycomb Music to host a listening party at acclaimed New York City nightclub Cielo. Back during the West End days, we paired two labels with a weekly party at Cielo called *Roots NYC*: West End and Louie Vega's Vega Records. I can't speak for Josh, but the March 2017 album listening party for *6.9.69* was a bit of a full circle moment for me. Like Mel always used to say: *nothing happens by accident*. On the morning of his birthday that year, I wrote Josh Milan an open letter:

> Today is a special day. Today, we celebrate the birthday of my mainest main man Josh Milan! Love this brother so much! On top of these birthday celebrations, today is also the CD release of his inspiring *6.9.69* album. I have to talk about the cover art. This cover brings me so much emotion. To all of us true fans, do you all realize that, until now, we have NEVER seen Josh alone on his own album, upfront, center and in his elevated place in our music world?

Until now, we've seen and heard Josh under many names and associations such as Phase II, Alexander Hope, Klubhead, Project MSC, Black Rascals, System VIII, the Colour Funky, Funky People, Stardust, Exit, In-Sync, the James Toney Jr. Project, Honeysweet, the Raw Honey Poets and I'm sure I'm missing more.

Most notably, Josh released music as part of the critically acclaimed duo Blaze alongside Kevin Hedge and later, as part of the fantastic Elements of Life band. For the latter association, Josh earned his first Grammy nomination, singing and co-writing on many of the songs on the *Louie Vega Starring. . . XXVIII* LP, produced by Grammy-award winning producer and friend Louie Vega. But today, this day, June 9th, to me, marks the beginning of it all. Why? Because this is Josh Milan reborn, finally alone and in a full circle moment, releasing his music on his own independent record label, walking on his own path, wearing his own crown. #SixNineSixtyNine

But as a funny sidebar: at Josh's request, his name doesn't appear on the cover. Talk about irony! lol I managed to add his name to the spine of the CD and he didn't mention or seem to put up a fuss over the slight mention of his name also on the CDs themselves. Hope he doesn't mind now that I've spilled the beans :) Anyway, I'm truly humbled to bear witness to my friend and brother in celebrating the worldwide release of his magnificent *6.9.69* double album. My sincere congratulations to you Josh. You did it!

Josh and I were remaining loyal to our grass roots efforts while taking cues from the wider music world (e.g., pairing and windowing). Our vision for Honeycomb Music has always been to re-introduce live instrumentation to dance music and Josh always wants to "put a little paint where it ain't."

Back at Mixtape Sessions, I really took these notions of pairing to heart. I arranged for several radio interviews, DJ gigs, and appearances to coincide with the 10th Anniversary of Mixtape Sessions. As it turned out, I was invited to DJ at Cielo, the same famed night club and I enjoyed swimming in familiar waters. *Nothing happens by accident.* Again, Mel was in my head.

On the stock market, music was being pulled into unchartered waters. In a 2018 *Forbes* article, author Cherie Hu explains:

> Historically, the music business and the financial community have not been comfortable partners. Creativity happens on its own timeline, and is difficult to align with a system that expects consistent returns.
>
> Yet, an increasing number of financial firms are forming alternative investment funds that frame independent and emerging artists as the next lucrative asset class, such as BlackRock's Alignment Artist Capital and AGI Partners' Unison Fund.

As paid streaming subscriptions continue to drive aggregate growth in recorded music revenues, industry insiders are cashing in specifically on performance royalties, which are paid to songwriters and composers every time their work is "broadcast" in public (including on streaming services). Within the music industry, publishers like Concord Music Group and Round Hill Music are acquiring legacy catalogs for unprecedented, multimillion-dollar prices. According to Billboard, a songwriter's catalog typically sells for 10 times its net publishing share (NPS), but that multiple has increased to 12x or even 16x in recent years amidst a seller's market. In response, some companies are even trying to launch IPOs for song royalties.

The Hipgnosis Songs Fund, a music IP investment company co-founded by veteran artist manager Merck Mercuriadis (previous clients include Iron Maiden, Elton John, Macy Gray and Mary J. Blige), is planning a £200 million listing on the London Stock Exchange later this year. Music production duo F.B.T. Productions is selling off up to 25 percent of their royalty share from rapper Eminem's pre-2013 catalog, and online royalty marketplace Royalty Exchange is helping to raise anywhere from US$11 million to $50 million to list the income stream directly to NASDAQ, under the moniker *Royalty Flow*.[59]

---

[59] Hu, C. (2018, January 4). Is Now Really The Best Time To Invest In Music Royalties? Forbes. Web:
https://www.forbes.com/sites/cheriehu/2018/01/04/is-now-really-the-best-time-to-invest-in-music-royalties/#1be9922b3c8e

Just like Apple used music to create an empire, online royalty marketplaces are using music to initiate an IPO and go public. In a different part of town off Wall Street, Spotify was bragging about its increasing value throughout 2017. Co-founder Daniel Ek had reason to brag though. Spotify had been valued at $8 billion, having already spent over a decade clearing up its debt via several rounds of fundraising.[60] By 2008, two years after launching, Spotify raised $21.5 million. The following year, they raised another $50 million. And on and on it went for the next few years. During these fundraising rounds, venture capitalists and investors engaged in debt/equity swaps, which converted Spotify's debt into shares that could be traded on the stock market. While reports that previous summer had Spotify valued at $8 billion, Ek bragged that the figure was closer to $13 billion. Spotify then bought a stake in China's Tencent Music Entertainment, which runs three huge music streaming services there. In return, Tencent purchased an equity stake in Spotify.[61] In 2016, Tencent, Dragoneer and Goldman Sachs lent Spotify $1 billion via convertible debt financing, which gave them the ability to eventually turn their loans into equity. Essentially, Spotify too acted as its own venture capitalist, converting its debt into equity.[62]

---

[60] Cuozzo, S., Weiss, L. (2017, February 15). Spotify signs massive lease at 4 World Trade Center. The New York Post. Web: https://nypost.com/2017/02/15/spotify-signs-massive-lease-at-4-world-trade-center/

[61] Walters, N. (2018, January 14). What Is Spotify's Valuation Right Now? The Motley Fool. Web: https://www.fool.com/investing/2018/01/14/what-is-spotifys-valuation-right-now.aspx

[62] Schleifer, T., Kafka, P. (2018, January 3). How Spotify solved a $1 billion debt problem that will help it IPO. Recode. Web: https://www.recode.net/2018/1/3/16847786/spotify-tpg-tencent-debt-dragoneer-ipo-music-streaming

But, many industry "experts" expected Spotify to implode. Do a simple Google search for Spotify in 2017 and most of these supposed experts painted a bleak picture, but it wasn't entirely media spin at work. From an outsider's perspective, Spotify was in fiscal trouble. Its net losses doubled the previous year to $600 million and unlike Apple, Spotify wasn't pairing its service with a physical device like an iPhone. However, Spotify knew it was seen as the leader. At the time, there were more than 100 million users signed up, 40 million of them paid subscribers to its premium tier.[63] To boot, Taylor Swift had seemingly squashed her beef with the service having made all of her albums available again by the summer of 2017. Spotify and Swift had kissed and made up and the benefit to artists were that they now got paid on free Spotify streams during the trial period. At the top of 2018, reports surfaced that the service was now worth a whopping $18 billion and was preparing itself to go public. Up until 2018, Spotify was a privately owned company, but with its plans to initiate an IPO, it was clear that Spotify had its sights set on becoming publicly owned and traded. I'm no stock market guru, but I understand that when a privately-owned company like Spotify goes public, an Initial Public Offering (IPO) is held. A traditional IPO allows the public to purchase shares via investment banks in an effort to raise funds. The rules around a traditional IPO are strict and would compromise the super voting majority power that co-founders Daniel Ek and Martin Lorentzon wanted to retain. In April 2018, Spotify circumvented the traditional IPO route and instead opted to engage in a "direct listing" on the New York Stock Exchange, allowing existing

---

[63] Plummer, R. (2017, February 12). The clock is ticking for Spotify. BBC News. Web: https://www.bbc.com/news/business-38930699

investors to sell shares without raising money from new ones. The move was also aimed at saving hundreds of millions in underwriting fees from investment banks. On the day it listed, Spotify was valued at $20 billion.[64]

This was a complete game changer, as you can imagine, but the big winners weren't just Ek and Lorentzon. We already knew that Sony, Universal Music Group and Warner Music had a stake in Spotify because of the leaks, but of course, the particulars are never voluntarily shared with the press. Because SEC rules require disclosure of shareholders with 5% or more ownership, it was revealed that Sony owned 5.7% of Spotify, while reports uncovered that the other two labels owned an estimated 4% each. These labels weren't just partners in a vague sense, they were co-owners and shareholders. Sony walked away with $1.5 billion and $1 billion for UMG and Warner, respectively.[65] Of course, the three majors each pledged to share with their artists any profit generated by the sales of the company's equity in Spotify, but without full transparency, there's no way of knowing how much, if any, were distributed to the artists. On a broader scale, we have converted music from art to a publicly traded commodity that is subject to the fluctuations, activities and shifts in value that the market dictates.

This is the gentrification of art on Wall Street.

---

[64] Reuters. (2017, September 28). Spotify Is Likely to IPO at a $20 Billion Valuation. Fortune. Web: http://fortune.com/2017/09/28/spotify-ipo-valuation/

[65] Variety Staff. (2018, April 3, 2018). Spotify: At Day's Close, What Are the Major Labels' Shares Worth? A Lot. Variety. Web: https://variety.com/2018/biz/news/spotify-at-days-close-what-are-sony-warner-and-universals-shares-worth-a-lot-1202743146/

Chapter 11: Art Goes Public

Whether you're accessing your favorite song online for free or not, corporations, in short time, have completely monopolized your music experience. The stories about Apple Music, Spotify, TIDAL, YouTube and other similar streaming services highlight this monopolization. In fact, music has really been privatized and placed behind a veneer of free public access. When we join social media and begin creating and sharing content, we think that we own that content and therefore, only we have the exclusive rights to exploit that content. When you agree to the terms and conditions during signup, you are allowing that platform to use and make money from your content with your consent. With a platform like YouTube, for example, Principal Attorney Daliah Saper explains:

> "YouTube always allows the owners to retain ownership of their work. But what they require in their terms of service is that you grant to YouTube a non-exclusive, worldwide, perpetual license to freely sub-license, re-distribute, re-publish, monetize, and whatever they may want to do with your video. They're basically requiring that you grant YouTube all of the same rights that you have with your video, short of turning over your rights to them" (i.e., assigning to YouTube your complete rights).[66]

---

[66] Crowell, G. (2011, February 3). Who Owns Your YouTube Video? You, YouTube, or Someone Else Entirely? Tubular Insights. Web: https://tinyurl.com/yc2mu4er

The corporation that owns that platform can also censor your content or completely deactivate your account based on what you say and what you're sharing.

Inevitably, corporations are attracted to consolidating their power in the marketplace. Look no further than the proposed Sinclair Broadcasting/Tribute Media merger as well as the proposed Time Warner/AT&T merger to understand that a consolidation like this means we're getting closer and closer to an over-reliance on one mode of music consumption (streaming) and one way to consume it (internet). For decades, music products came in various forms and most of it at the same time: vinyl, 8-track, cassette tape, CD, download, and stream. Today, only streaming is left. We've placed so much value on this one mode of consumption, but have completely overlooked the thin line we've created. Try not paying your Internet and phone bills for a while; your services will get disconnected. Once that happens, you'll start to get a real sense of how little music you're able to access because you don't have an Internet connection nor a working device.

Our ability to access the Internet is completely dependent upon corporations. Comcast, AT&T, Verizon, Time Warner and other such Internet service providers have slowly monopolized telecommunications in our world, not unlike what we're witnessing in the music business. Up until recently, the transmission of data was treated equally on the Internet and an open Internet order kept the Internet neutral. This is called "net neutrality." What do I mean? When net neutrality is enforced, all Internet service providers must allow equal access to apps and content, regardless of the source. If it were not enforced, your Internet service provider could make it harder for you to access parts of the Internet at its own discretion. Without the assurance of net neutrality, large Internet companies could favor their own business interests. Net neutrality effects everything from Internet speed to overall access.

Most of the summer and fall of 2017 was spent talking about net neutrality, but by December, the Federal Communications Commission voted to repeal. The repeal vote happened so quickly, but the actual process of de-neutralizing the Internet is slow and long, which might be a good thing if you take a look at our rural and poorer communities, for instance. In these communities, the repeal of net neutrality has an even stronger impact. Already, data from Pew Research shows that:

> . . . a little over half of American adults with household incomes under $30,000 have a home broadband connection, and one in three have a smartphone. This is why in 2016, the FCC modernized the Lifeline program, which gives low-income Americans a monthly $9.25 subsidy for communications services. Created during the Reagan administration and expanded during George W. Bush's presidency, Lifeline historically applied only to landline, and then mobile, phone service. The 2016 FCC modernization established structures for more efficient administration and mechanisms to spur competition among providers. It mandated the creation of a National Lifeline Eligibility Verifier system to ensure that only those eligible to receive Lifeline do so.

And it carefully began to shift the Lifeline subsidy to include broadband Internet access. FCC chair Ajit Pai has portrayed the Lifeline program and the people who benefit from it as hopelessly corrupt. Now he is proposing to make changes that will, for all intents and purposes, destroy the program. He aims to severely reduce both the supply of and demand for Lifeline-supported services.

One of Pai's first acts as chair was to chill competition and innovation in the Lifeline program. Pai reversed a decision made by former FCC chair Tom Wheeler that allowed nine new Lifeline providers into the program. In the process, Pai got rid of new competitors who could drive down prices and improve services.

Now, Pai proposes to limit Lifeline even further. Eliminating a Wheeler-era designation that welcomed new broadband providers into the program, the FCC said in December, will "better reflect the structure, operation, and goals of the Lifeline program." But if the goal of the program is to ensure that low-income Americans have affordable access to broadband, reducing competition in the program will do the exact opposite.

It gets worse. Pai proposes to make the Lifeline subsidy available only to those companies that own their facilities, like the wires, towers, and other infrastructure that make up networks. The problem here?

Seventy-five percent of Lifeline customers get their service from businesses that resell the capacity of companies like Sprint and T-Mobile. When the FCC opened the Lifeline subsidy to mobile phones back in 2008, these resellers came roaring into the market, increasing competition and reducing prices so that many subscribers pay little or nothing for service. Eliminating the carriers favored by three-quarters of the market will ensure that Lifeline prices will increase and quality of service will decrease. If resellers are forced out of the Lifeline program, some low-income Americans may find themselves unable to use their Lifeline subsidy at all. This result could have dire consequences—some Lifeline customers may find themselves without access to critical services like 911.[67]

This is the gentrification of art on the Internet.

So . . . is anybody fighting against this? Absolutely. You should know that at the time of the printing of this book, nearly two dozen state attorneys general have asked a federal court to reinstate net neutrality, arguing that the Federal Communications Commission failed to properly consider the aforementioned issues when removing the policy in 2017.

Net Neutrality activists have driven the fight to Washington, taking the FCC to court for their decision to repeal.

---

[67] Sohn, G., Fazlullah, A. (2018, February 21). Ajit Pai's Plan Will Take Broadband Away from Poor People. Wired. Web: https://www.wired.com/story/ajit-pais-plan-will-take-broadband-away-from-poor-people/

What this means is that your local and state officials are doing most of the fighting for you at the moment by filing briefs, arguing case law and critiquing the processes for reviewing and voting on these matters. What can you do? If you live in a state where your state attorney general is not 1 of the 22 state attorneys general currently in the fight, call them and your members of congress to urge them to join the fight to reinstate net neutrality. You'd be surprised what your local municipalities are up to in terms of community issues like this.

In short: **get involved and vote**! Contact your local officials, inquire about the issues that matter to you and your community, and pay close attention to what's happening to art in your community and around the world.

While you're registering to vote and then voting, keep in mind that Congress has finally stepped in to address lost royalty income, streaming songs that are older than 1972 and giving engineers and mixers an administrator to pay them their royalties. Let me explain.

On April 25, 2018, the U.S. House of Representatives passed a bill to address the matters I just mentioned, calling it the Music Modernization Act (MMA). You see, when it comes to unclaimed income for performance royalties (each time your music is performed publicly), ASCAP, BMI or SESAC in the states administer these royalties and add that income to the account you're registered for. When it comes to mechanical royalties (i.e., the money record labels and publishers earn from each stream), streaming companies are required to submit a Notice of Intention with the U.S. Copyright Office.

An NOI formally recognizes that a specific streamer has royalties it is trying to pay, but is unable to locate the correct rights holders.

When you consider the sheer volume of daily streams, you can only imagine how inundated with NOIs the U.S. Copyright Office is. The Music Modernization Act mandates the creation of a reporting body to administer unclaimed mechanical royalties. Reports indicate that the MLC or the Mechanical License Collective will be created as a means for streamers like Spotify and Apple Music to correctly distribute the more than $1.5 billion in suspended income (unclaimed royalties). Within the MMA is the CLASSICS Act (also known as the Compensating Legacy Artists for their Songs, Service, & Important Contributions to Society Act). This act requires digital services to pay both rights holders and artists for the use of recordings made before 1972.

For non-interactive streamers like iHeartRadio, Pandora, Music Match, online radio stations and the biggest of them all, SiriusXM Radio, the CLASSICS Act means they'll have to pay more when they're already fighting to pay less. These non-interactive streaming companies have to pay a smaller royalty rate to license our music than interactive streaming companies. The Copyright Royalty Board (CRB) ultimately sets the statutory royalty rate for ad-based commercial non-interactive webcasters at $0.0017 starting in 2016, and rising in subsequent years to account for inflation. For SiriusXM, this was a huge jump from 11.5% of their revenue share to 15.5%. They fought the CRB as a result of the ruling and were vocal in their opposition of the Music Modernization Act while appealing. The way that the appeals process works is first a licensee must ask the

CRB to review its rate determination and, if the board decides to uphold the rates, then the licensee can take its case to an appeals court. SiriusXM had already put in a motion requesting a review of its 2018-2022 rates and while the CRB has not yet indicated whether it would review the appeal, let alone change the rates, when it responded to that motion it said it was interested in hearing feedback on why the rate should remain at 15.5 percent of revenue or be lowered to 14.7 percent for the next five years. Some saw that response as an early indication that the CRB was open to lowering Sirius' rate. As passage of the Music Modernization Act on the Senate side neared, everyone involved seemed to be scrambling for compromise especially in light of the bill being 'fast-tracked' in order to pass it during the session and before the midterm elections.

With this latest compromise incorporated into the law, the appeal won't happen and SiriusXM will have the same 15.5% of revenue rate through 2027 – a victory for SiriusXM. Simply put: they kicked the problem down the road nine years just like they did in 1998. For producers, engineers and mixers who strike direct deals with artists, the Music Modernization Act is a victory for them as well. As a reminder: SoundExchange, a CRB-appointed non-profit organization, collects and distributes digital performance royalties on behalf of recording artists, master rights owners (like record labels), and independent artists who own their masters. The proposed AMP Act creates a way for producers and engineers to receive direct payments from SoundExchange when recordings are used on satellite radio and online radio services like Pandora. This is great news for engineers, mixers and producers as it removes the honor system between artist and producer.

On September 19, 2018, the Senate unanimously passed the Music Modernization Act. From there, the bill went back to the House of Representatives to get re-approved based on the revised version of the bill. On October 11, 2018, President Trump signed the Music Modernization Act into law, officially passing the most sweeping reform to copyright law in decades.[68]

We also can't discuss all of this music modernization without addressing the public spaces where much of this music is consumed. Venues, nightclubs, outdoor parks and mixed-use art spaces are essential spots for music to survive. After all, the digital landscape directly impacts the physical landscape. Let's examine the tragic *Ghost Ship* fire case for a moment. On the night of December 2, 2016, a fire broke out at the long-running *Ghost Ship*, an art space in Oakland, California that functioned as both cultural performance space and housing for artists, poets, performers, musicians and other creatives. The fire killed 36 people and caused a ripple effect in the art space community, writ large. To be fair, the *Ghost Ship* warehouse was uniquely dangerous, described by some as a "tinderbox" and a "deathtrap." Derick Almena, who managed the 10,000 square-foot industrial space, had constructed dwellings inside without proper approvals, charging tenants anywhere from $300 to $1,400 to live there.[69]

---

[68] Christman, E. (2018, September 19). Music Modernization Act Passes Senate: Should End Confusion on SiriusXM Pre-1972 Settlement. Billboard. Web: https://www.billboard.com/articles/business/8476042/music-modernization-act-passes-senate-siriusxm-pre-1972

[69] Levin, S. (2018, August 9). Evictions and 'criminalized spaces': the legacy of Oakland's Ghost Ship fire. The Guardian. Web: https://www.theguardian.com/us-news/2018/aug/09/oakland-ghost-ship-fire-sentencing-evictions-deaths

Others claimed that the owners of the building rented a space, knowing it was dangerous and unsuitable for leasing. What happened next is very alarming.

Three days after the *Ghost Ship* fire and only 22 minutes away in Richmond, California, "tenants of *Burnt Ramen*, a local underground punk venue and residential warehouse, were put on notice by city officials that they could be targeted due to unsafe conditions. Their friends' funerals had not yet happened when news cameras showed up at their door in Richmond, a city just north of Oakland. Soon, they were evicted and forced to live out of their cars and on couches."[70]

Over two years later, the *Burnt Ramen* community is still fighting. So, on the one hand, you can't blame municipalities from taking action in light of tragic fires. I remember *Happy Land*. Do you? The *Happy Land* fire was an act of arson that killed 87 people trapped in the unlicensed *Happy Land* social club in the Bronx on March 25, 1990. Most of the victims were young Hondurans celebrating Carnival, many of them part of the Garifuna American community. The fire sparked passionate debates about dangerous gathering spaces with only one way in and one way out. We must remain safe while enjoying art. There are no if, ands, or buts about that. The other consideration is the gentrification of art in these municipalities. In the name of safety, art spaces in our communities are being wiped out.

---

[70] Levin, S. (2018, August 9). Evictions and 'criminalized spaces': the legacy of Oakland's Ghost Ship fire. The Guardian. Web: https://www.theguardian.com/us-news/2018/aug/09/oakland-ghost-ship-fire-sentencing-evictions-deaths

The continued *Burnt Ramen* fights are proof that Richmond officials aren't eager to relocate these tenants and Richmond, as a result, has become devoid of the art community that many came to depend on.

> As rent prices skyrocket in major cities like Oakland, urban artist communities are already vulnerable to displacement. Of the tenants who survived the *Ghost Ship* fire, many were forced to leave the city for lack of cheap housing options. Others were subjected to living spaces more neglected than the warehouse (many renters under-report dangerous building conditions for fear of eviction). The fire raised questions about the future of DIY venues, which operate on volunteer efforts and minimal funds. Without the cooperation of local law enforcement, which previously had a habit of looking the other way, landlords would rather evict their tenants than pay for expensive repairs and zoning licenses. Despite Oakland Mayor Libby Schaaf's promise to protect these spaces with Executive Order 2017-1: "Improving Safety for Non-Permitted Spaces While Avoiding Displacement," few landlords have come forward to offer their properties for inspection. Instead, venues around the country like Purple 33 in Los Angeles were shut down briskly and without much notice.[71]

This is the gentrification of art on Main Street.

---

[71] Macdougall, K. (2018, March 1). Oakland's Ghost Ship Fire: How Cities Have Responded to Art Spaces One Year Later. MXDWN. Web: https://music.mxdwn.com/2018/03/01/features/oaklands-ghost-ship-fire-how-cities-have-responded-to-art-spaces-one-year-later/

Being a house head from Jersey has its benefits. For lovers of this kind of dance music, New Jersey is the place to be, especially during the summer months when several outdoor events are free to attend and bring out thousands of house heads, each ready to dance from noon to 10 p.m. With it being such a short trip over the Hudson River from NYC, Newark and surrounding Northern New Jersey cities have become a major destination for house music festivals. The Lincoln Park Coast Cultural District is considered the *grandfather* of these house music festivals due to its immensely impactful 3-day Lincoln Park Music Festival. Annually, LPCCD hosts a genre of music each day. The first day of the festival highlights Gospel and Jazz music. The second day highlights House music and the third highlights Hip Hop. Running for over a dozen years, this particular festival has become the model for others who aspire to host their own outdoor festival. Within the context of house music, the effects are undeniable. Since Lincoln Park's festival, over half a dozen others in New Jersey alone have emerged. There's even one organization that developed its own 3-day festival, but devoted it entirely to house music! I had been fortunate enough to be invited by LPCCD to play their festival one year (on day 2 of course) and had a ball. As a DJ, there's little greater feeling than the gratification of witnessing a sea of happy faces and dancing bodies enjoying your live set. For a DJ, these moments are as close as a DJ can get to the connection that fans feel with their artist's new music. It's the glue that I mentioned earlier. All of these festivals are a celebration of a wonderful style of music we feel so compelled to keep alive. I shudder to think of what this house music community would do if a situation arose like *Burnt Ramen* where our dance spaces would end up in danger of closing.

Oh wait . . . this has already happened. Christian, a DJ acquaintance of mine, talks with me about this sometimes. There was a time when he would patronize a series of nightclubs throughout the course of a night. He'd criss cross Newark, patronizing nightclubs like Zanzibar, Club America, The Docks and Paradisio.

Then, he'd hit up numerous, smaller bars and dance spaces that catered to house music. Spots he frequented include: New Experience, Studio 7, Mr. West, Metro Galaxy, Cowboys, Murphy's, Club Shanique, Club Hardware and Tweed. Sadly, none of these establishments exist today. Combine corporatization, gentrification, rising rents and changing attitudes about local music and you'll have your answer as to why these venues no longer exist. Newark's outdoor festivals of today are arguably a new incarnation of the nightclubs of yesteryear. But one big difference sticks out: these festivals are free to attend, but dance spaces normally charge to get in, so where's the business? In a Venn diagram, *free* and *pay* would be written inside two overlapping circles. The intersection (known as the overlapping area) between *free* and *pay* is where the solution resides. In this discussion, it's important to draw from what's happening in the wider music world. In streaming music, for example, it might be worth examining the *freemium* model. What would happen if those Newark festivals I mentioned provided free access for a time period and then charged a fee to get in after that? What would happen if free entrance was granted with the purchase of a product ala pairing? In my head, I kept asking myself: what would happen if a paid event were paired with community outreach?

Enter D. Wild Music Radio.

I met DJ, producer and break dancer extraordinaire Duce Martinez back when I was working at Axiom Studios. He's an effective connector of people with an uncanny ability to bring individuals and groups together in the spirit of collaboration. Years after Axiom, Duce began hosting Friday night get-togethers in his Newark apartment, DJing long marathon sets into the wee hours of the morning. Ralphie Boy Muniz, a mutual friend, reconnected us by inviting me to join him, Duce and Cilla, a friend of Ralph's, to host a talk segment during Duce's Friday night set. We all immediately connected with each other during these talk shows. Funny enough, without any prompting, we all took on certain characters or personas while talking on the mic. Ralph was our anchor, steering the conversation and keeping things flowing; Cilla had impeccable comedic timing while providing the female perspective; Duce was the "wild card" on the mic (never knowing what he'd do or say) and I was the nerdy news guy, bringing up music business topics (surprise surprise!)

The interest in these Friday night soirees grew fast over time and other DJs began jockeying for guest spots on Friday nights. Duce invited Ralph, Cilla and I to form a radio station together, aptly called "D. Wild Music Radio." The "D" obviously stands for Duce and the "wild" describes the zany atmosphere we all created on Friday nights as well as Duce's naturally energetic personality. In the interest of community outreach, I pushed for the station to be more than a place to hear music. I wanted to be involved with something that was altruistic and D. Wild became a platform for pairing music with DJ culture and community service. Before we knew it, those guest DJs became part of a roster of several programmers we invited to join the station.

We developed a daily schedule, designed a logo, published a website, signed up for a broadcasting platform for live streaming and chatting, used our on-air personalities and social media tools to attract listeners and paired milestones with events. Duce's birthday became a DJ showcase at the Winter Music Conference in Miami where we all took turns playing at Sushi Samba. An attempt at building awareness for the station and our DJs became an annual NYC boat ride. With this annual boat ride, we paired DJ appearances with a headlining performance. We signed up as a team to walk in our local Suicide Prevention and Domestic Violence Awareness walks, sponsored webinars during Autism Awareness month, and hosted annual toy drives during the holidays.

Ralph and Cilla eventually left the station, but Duce and I continued on, adding programmers and initiatives. Personally, I turned those Friday night news segments into a talk show for the station and leveraged that show to broadcast on terrestrial radio in Africa, thanks to my old friend Taha at Capital Radio, who I introduced to you earlier. Today, D. Wild Music Radio has grown to 32 programmers and hundreds of fans from around the globe. Just recently, D. Wild surpassed its 1.3 millionth listen!

I need to be honest about something though. Yes, D. Wild fulfills that sense of altruism in me, but it also fills a need to create my own DJ opportunities. I suppose it feeds a part of the ego that all DJs have. At the moment, I'm not getting booked as a touring DJ (a goal of mine) and as a result, I don't get to play often. By developing a station with Duce, I was able to create opportunities to play as a DJ or perform as a recording artist.

I take these opportunities seriously and DJ like it is going to be my last chance to ever play. The crowds have been so gracious. I also use the platform to broadcast and promote my own releases, inviting Mixtape Sessions' recording artists to perform. Through this work, we've managed to DJ in some unique places. Nearly every Halloween, we're invited to perform and DJ on a float for NYC's annual Halloween parade in Greenwich Village. Nearly every year, we are invited to DJ for the Central Park Skaters' Association. From boat rides to festivals, our participation makes me happy which makes it all worthwhile. I get quite a bit of spiritual, emotional and fiscal fulfillment from these experiences. Some are paid gigs and some are not, but I keep thinking about that Venn diagram and let it be a guide for making good business decisions. The same principles apply for our work at Honeycomb. A website launch is paired with the launch of a weekly Internet radio show. Josh's birthday is paired with an annual boat ride and a debut solo album release. Josh and I also apply that Venn diagram concept to releases. For instance, we'll offer a full-length album entirely for free and pair that free release with a holiday. In Honeycomb's case, Josh produced several of these albums and Honeycomb Music released them as free downloads. A 9-track Christmas album and an 18-track Black History album are just examples. What did we get in return? In order to download or stream the album, you had to give your email address. We collect those email addresses and then occasionally email announcements. Each year, we try new and creative ways at D. Wild to create more opportunities while pairing those opportunities with community service. In the summer of 2017, we reached a turning point as a new chapter began in the station's story.

The Newark Public Library invited Duce and I to host an outdoor DJ dance party in their courtyard on Friday nights. Take a moment and think about the symbolism of this invitation. Through our community work, we end up getting involved with a library, the epicenter for community-based resources. It happens to be the Newark Public Library. This is the same city with a plethora of places to go for free during the summertime. And it happens to be on Friday nights, the beginning of it all for D. Wild Music Radio. I heard Mel in my head again.

Nothing happens by accident.

The Library Music Sessions turned out to be the perfect event for us. We launched in June 2017, the first summer after a tumultuous election where factors including the lack of voting caused a dramatic political shift in the country. The one thing I could do to help was to bring attention to voting as a right worth exercising. During our Friday night sessions, we partnered with the library to make resource tables available for our attendees-- a small, but burgeoning crowd. Throughout the night, we would announce and promote these available library resources: *Earn your G.E.D.! Register to vote! Learn to read! Get a library card! Get involved!*

Then Hurricane Maria happened, decimating Puerto Rico, the U.S. Virgin Islands, Barbuda, Dominica, St. Martin and other vulnerable areas. Instantly, there were pop-up events in support of relief efforts everywhere. Our phones blew up from calls from our programmers, asking what we were going to do in response. Immediately, Duce and I used Friday nights at the library to host a donations drive. We were a drop off location for weeks.

Some of our programmers collaborated with D. Wild to host their own relief events. Before we knew it, we were quickly learning about pallets, palletizing, trucks, planes, shipments, the Jones Act, efforts from local municipalities and an endless amount more. I couldn't be prouder of our collective efforts. I even got to apply my own agenda about being transparent by posting pictures of us physically dropping off donations, receipts of our donations, pictures to verify shipment of goods and live video to maintain accountability. We worked transparently with car dealerships, local municipalities, fitness centers, boxing clubs, bars, and the Newark Public Library, of course. The following summer, Duce and I were invited back to the library. We were astonished that word had spread all last summer about *The Library Music Sessions* and that our small, but thriving crowd had grown into a massive event. During the summer of 2018, we hosted a thousand guests or more each week. It was the kind of party that started full and then swelled in the blink of an eye. You know you're getting a lot of notice when superstar DJs start showing up to check you and the crowd out. Taking a step back for a moment, I often wonder why the music business isn't more willing to support more transparency given the ever-changing landscape we find ourselves in. Much like in the library experience, the music business could learn better ways to collaboratively market, pair music with community service, increase incomes and still advocate for more openness. In essence, Honeycomb Music and Mixtape Sessions are labels that strongly utilize the concepts of pairing and windowing. In terms of our work at D. Wild Music Radio, we're combining pairing with altruism. All of this was influenced by what's occurring in the music business today. So what would I envision to help address some of the issues plaguing the music business?

Again, I envision a simple and transparent system between artists that negates the effects of manual interplay. For the most part, artists tend to get signed to major and minor deals based on the fundamental premise that one entity gets the money. The artist then agrees to let that entity determine and issue a royalty statement, and subsequently distribute earned royalties to the artist. The entity can be a record label, a music publisher or even another independent artist. This structure mandates that one receives the funds and then shares the funds to the other. The crippling issue is the 'honor system' that artists are left to enact in this arrangement. What artists need the most is a simple way to navigate the system that removes the need to enact an honor system. As artists, we are eager to manage our earnings within a central, one-stop shop for administering our publishing income, digital performance income, licensing income and mechanical royalties; and it should all be open-sourced and transparent for all parties to see and analyze. With their business affairs in order, artists will be free to explore greater connection between music and health. A connection worth pondering is music as therapy. As part of the grieving process, I used music to deal with my dad's death, my mother's ovarian cancer diagnosis, my eccentric college experiences, my wedding day, the birth of our son, the adoption of our daughters, the death of the Godfather of Disco, and from the light of the day to the dark of the night. Music is a healer, but it's not considered medicine nor is it placed within the lanes of medical research nor of psychiatry. What if royalties were paid to artists for songs used in a medical or psychiatric setting? What about a prescription of music? Don't care for this scenario? Ok, but let's at least talk about how to think innovatively about the future of music royalties.

As a reminder, music royalties are paid to record labels and music publishers who then pay the artists based on the agreement. We must innovate and evolve past this power dynamic as well. We must demand transparency from these record companies and music publishers just like we're demanding it from streaming companies. Earlier in the book, I promised I would explain a bit more about music as a public utility model. Back in 2005 and during the David Kusek days, the staff at West End was invited to attend a talk at the Learning Annex given by Grammy Award-winning producer L.A. Reid. He spoke about his career, advice for new producers and the future of music. During the question and answer portion, I raised my hand early and high, dying to ask for his thoughts on music as a public utility model. He immediately conflated public utility for a subscription model and I felt frustrated at what I deemed was a pivot. In hindsight, I don't really blame him. I can easily conflate the two myself. In a setting where music operates as a public utility, music is accessed much like water or electricity. Open the faucet and out pours an unlimited supply of the public utility that is music. Exactly like a subscription service, you would pay a monthly fee, but not to the streaming service, rather to the Internet Service Provider. Then, that ISP would be regulated by Congress so as to avoid telecommunications companies from engaging in throttling, blocking, and slowing down the data transmission from a competitor or adversary. Additionally, music as a public utility would place a protection on costs so that companies couldn't charge what they wanted, whenever they wanted. Um . . . that already happened. As it turns out, had we converted music into a public utility model, the same company that controls your ability to connect to the Internet would quite literally be the same company that controls your ability to access music.

We must free the music business from the corporate models that devalue music and earn artists a fraction of a penny per stream while giant companies grow larger off the backs of those artists. Music must be placed in the fiscal winners' circle among the digital advertisers, streaming services and user-generated content platforms that earn billions and trillions. If I could make a prediction, it is that music distributors or digital music aggregators will begin to lose strength as artists will be looking to strike direct deals with streaming services as a way of circumventing the cumbersome corporate approach. Even recently, Spotify announced a new beta feature that will allow independent artists to upload their music directly to the platform instead of through a label or digital aggregator.

> Normally, artists who aren't signed to a major label have to pay a fee to a third-party service like Tunecore to upload their music to Spotify. The new upload feature won't work like SoundCloud, where songs can be instantly available. Instead, Spotify views it as a way for artists to have control over their own music in advance of its release date. Those who are part of the program will be shown an interface where they can upload their music and accompanying artwork, pick a release day, input additional information (like if it's a single or an album), and then preview how it will look once published. Direct upload is being offered as a free service.[72]

[72] Deahl, D. (2018, September 20). Spotify will now let artists directly upload their music to the platform. The Verge. Web: https://www.theverge.com/2018/9/20/17879840/spotify-artist-direct-upload-independent-music

Spotify, in taking a huge leap like this, will once again change the music business landscape and improve the income levels for artists. But, you have to wonder: if large aggregators start losing their power, how might they lobby to consolidate that power? Either way you slice it: we, the artists, no longer want a fraction of a penny per stream. We want a livable wage. We want ownership in our destiny and freedom to engage in de-corporatization, if we wish.

As my *Freedom Radio Hour* collaborator, Eddie Nicholas, always says: "we should be getting at least 50%!" I hear you, Eddie!

So, how much are most of these platforms paying out?

From highest to lowest, read 'em and weep:

Microsoft's Groove Music *(now defunct)* = $0.02730 per stream
Napster (listed as Rhapsody) = $0.01682 per stream
TIDAL = $0.01284 per stream
Apple Music = $0.00783 per stream
Deezer = $0.00624 per stream
Google Play = $0.00611 per stream
Spotify = $0.00397 per stream
Pandora = $0.00134 per stream
YouTube = $0.00074 per stream[73]

Abysmal, right? As I learn more about what all of this means, I prepare to send the next round of royalty statements to our artists and pay them.

---

[73] Sanchez, D. (2018, January 16). What Streaming Music Services Pay (Updated for 2018). Digital Music News. Web: https://www.digitalmusicnews.com/2018/01/16/streaming-music-services-pay-2018/

AUTHOR'S BIO

Adam Cruz is a DJ, artist, writer, record label executive, graphic designer and music business enthusiast. Adam has made dance floors groove to his expansive collection of music and his spirited DJing style for years. Heavily influenced by such legendary DJs and producers as Frankie Feliciano, Doug Smith, Nicky P., Louie Vega and so many others, Adam has taken the house music community by storm, producing and playing great music from around the globe. Not surprisingly, his passion for music has garnered respect and admiration from his musical peers for years.

Adam's innovative approach has been heard from Washington D.C.'s Five Club and Club Red to London's SoshoMatch and Notting Hill Arts Club. Back across the globe in New York City, Adam has been heard at Bang the Party, Sole Channel, and Roots alongside Kevin Hedge and Grammy Award-winner, "Little Louie" Vega.

For almost four years, Adam dedicated his time to playing at Brooklyn's Halcyon, where his party, Mixtape Sessions, took on a new venue and voice for house music, playing alongside such artists and DJs as Louie Vega, Blaze, Tony Humphries, Jellybean Benitez, DJ Mr. V, Frankie Feliciano, and many others.

Concurrently and after Halcyon closed its doors at 227 Smith Street, Adam began broadcasting his interviews from that Brooklyn café over the Internet. Aptly calling it "Mixtape Sessions," Adam was one of the first DJs in his community to host an online radio show.

Having been a DJ since he was 10 years old, it's no surprise that his love of music led him to work directly with historic dance music label MAW Records for producing duo Masters at Work ("Little Louie" Vega and Kenny "Dope" Gonzalez) and later, with the legendary disco label West End Records, founded by disco pioneer Mel Cheren (called "The Godfather of Disco").

In 2004, Adam became the A&R and Production Director for that illustrious label and in 2009, he was appointed Vice President. Adam has signed over 50 musical copyrights, co-produced a documentary film about Mel Cheren, and worked with producers and artists from all over the world, including: Blaze, MAW, DJ Spinna, hip-hop pioneers Marley Marl and Red Alert, and many others.

Today, Adam runs his own record label, Mixtape Sessions, and Honeycomb Music, alongside longtime music partner Josh Milan. From time to time, he also dabbles in art, having recently developed a graphic art series, entitled "Plena Punk," exploring his questions around Puerto Rican identity.

For Mixtape Sessions, Adam has released his third *Freedom* LP, a fantastic follow up to his critically acclaimed *Emospiritual Travelin* LP. As a producer, he has built a solid reputation for his creative production style and song-writing prowess. Adam has recorded with award-winning artists such as Eddie Nicholas, Flora Cruz, Gerideau, Lillias White, Manchildblack, queen AaMinah, and several others. As a DJ, he spins an energetic blend of Jazz, Funk, Latin, and soulful Dance music to a solid base of loyal listeners.

For several seasons now, he and co-host Eddie Nicholas have been discussing music business news and trends from around the globe on the "Freedom Radio Hour," broadcasting weekly on Capital Radio 91.6FM The Heartbeat of Sudan in Africa and on the web at: dwildmusicradio.com.

Adam earned his B.A. in Creative Arts & Technology - Music Technology from Bloomfield College and has been a voting member of The Recording Academy since 2006. He currently resides in Bloomfield, New Jersey with his wife and three children.

Visit freedomradiohour.com and watch/listen to the Freedom Radio Hour - your #1 source for music business news and trends from around the globe! FREE app available now for Android and iPhone users - search 'freedom radio hour' within your phone's app store and stay informed!

djadamcruz.com

freedomradiohour.com

mixtapesessions.com

BOOK EDITOR'S BIO

Amanda Frontany is an educator who has served the New York City public school system for more than 22 years. For the past 18 years, she has taught grades 8-12 at Medgar Evers College Preparatory School in Crown Heights, Brooklyn. She is a College Board-authorized teacher of Advanced Placement English Language & Composition and Advanced Placement Capstone (AP Seminar & AP Research). Amanda has a Bachelor's Degree in Communications and English from New York University, a Master's Degree in English Education from New York University, and an Advanced Certificate in School District Administration & Supervision from SUNY Stony Brook.

She is a NYC Teacher-Mentor for new teachers, a curriculum writer, and a professional development facilitator. Outside of education, Amanda is a freelance writer and editor. She highlights soulful music artists, musicians, producers, and DJs through her interview website, Questions & Artists, at: questionsandartists.com

Amanda currently resides in Crown Heights, Brooklyn with her husband and two sons.

BOOK DESIGNER'S BIO

Jose Gonzalez is a Multimedia/Interactive Designer. Born in the 1970's, he was heavily influenced by Graffiti Art and learned the majority of his design principles from the art form. His passion for design landed him at Arts High School in Newark, NJ where he developed proper skills in acrylics, papier-mâché, clay sculpting, photography and art history. Today, with over 30 years of design experience, Jose has a Bachelor of Science in Multimedia Design and Management with a great deal of skills in Adobe Creative Cloud and UX/UI Design in both PC, Mac and drawing tablets. He still prefers to sketch out ideas in his traditional art setting: pencil and paper.

Jose is also a fantastic DJ, producer and record label owner. Take a listen to Fresh Sol Music at: www.traxsource.com/label/1961/fresh-sol-music

He currently resides in New Jersey with his wife and two children.

jose1972@verizon.net
www.be.net/Gonzalez1972
Twitter: JoseFreshSol

BIBLIOGRAPHY

Aguiar, L., Martens, B. (2013, March 21). Digital Music Consumption on the Internet: Evidence from Clickstream Data. Contrefaçon Riposte. Web: http://www.contrefacon-riposte.info/publications/4180-digital-music-consumption-on-the-Internet-evidence-from-clickstream-data

Al-Greene, B. (2012, December 20). YouTube in 2012: A Year of Expansion and Experiments. Mashable. Web: https://mashable.com/2012/12/20/youtube-milestones-2012/#qh3qmoGT1Zql

Allen, S. (2018, September 14). Has Pandora Stock Peaked? Market Realist. Web: https://marketrealist.com/2018/09/has-pandora-stock-peaked

Apple Press Info (2013). iTunes Store Sets New Record with 25 Billion Songs Sold. Apple, Inc. Web: http://www.apple.com/pr/library/2013/02/06iTunes-Store-Sets-New-Record-with-25-Billion-Songs-Sold.html

Asktrakhan, I. (2016, May 17). 2 billion people worldwide are unbanked – here's how to change this. Web: https://www.weforum.org/agenda/2016/05/2-billion-people-worldwide-are-unbanked-heres-how-to-change-this

Atkinson, C. (2017, October 20). Billboard Magazine Won't Add YouTube Views Into Its Album Charts. NBC News. Web: https://www.nbcnews.com/pop-culture/music/billboard-magazine-won-t-add-youtube-views-its-album-charts-n812331

Beatport News (2010). Becoming 'One': Anatomy of a #1 hit. Beatport.com. Web: http://news.beatport.com/blog/2010/07/06/becoming-one-anatomy-of-a-1-hit

BMI (2017). Types of Copyright. Web: https://www.bmi.com/licensing/entry/types_of_copyrights

Bradshaw, T. (2011, July 14). Spotify launches in the US. Financial Times. Web: https://www.ft.com/content/0d602d7c-adf9-11e0-a2ab-00144feabdc0

Caulfield, K. (2017, December 5). U2's 'Songs of Experience' Heading for No. 1 on Billboard 200 Albums Chart. Billboard. Web: https://www.billboard.com/articles/columns/chart-beat/8061700/u2-songs-of-experience-heading-no-1-billboard-200

Chaffin, J., Allison, K. (2006, May 1). Apple sets tune for pricing of song downloads. Financial Times. Web: https://goo.gl/Fz8K4n

Chart History. (2006, December 9). Save A Place On The Dance Floor for Me Promo Only: Underground Club (January 2007). Billboard. Web: http://www.billboard.com/artist/300537/dawn-tallman/chart

Chen, B. (2010, April 28). April 28, 2003: Apple Opens iTunes Store. Wired. Web: https://goo.gl/DkVudQ

Christman, E. (2018, September 19). Music Modernization Act Passes Senate: Should End Confusion on SiriusXM Pre-1972 Settlement. Billboard. Web: https://www.billboard.com/articles/business/8476042/music-modernization-act-passes-senate-siriusxm-pre-1972

Cormier, R. (2014, July 8). 15 Albums That Cost a Fortune to Make. Mental Floss. Web: https://goo.gl/Xys8U3

Cox, J. (2016, February 5). Rihanna, the RIAA, and making a platinum record in 2016. The Verge. Web: https://www.theverge.com/2016/2/5/10923826/rihanna-anti-platinum-album-riaa-streaming-2016

Crowell, G. (2011, February 3). Who Owns Your YouTube Video? You, YouTube, or Someone Else Entirely? Tubular Insights. Web: http://tubularinsights.com/youtube-copyright-ownership/

Cruz, A. (2006). The Future of House Music: Digitizing the Global Dance Floor. New York: Listen Magazine.

Cruz, A. (2014, January 2). 5 Things All House Music Artists Can Learn From Beyoncé's Surprise LP. Freedom Radio Hour. Web: http://news.freedomradiohour.com/2014/01/5-things-all-house-music-artists-can.html

Cuozzo, S., Weiss, L. (2017, February 15). Spotify signs massive lease at 4 World Trade Center. The New York Post. Web: https://nypost.com/2017/02/15/spotify-signs-massive-lease-at-4-world-trade-center/

Deahl, D. (2018, September 20). Spotify will now let artists directly upload their music to the platform. The Verge. Web: https://www.theverge.com/2018/9/20/17879840/spotify-artist-direct-upload-independent-music

DeAngelo, J. (2004, May 28). Billboard Sours on Prince's Musicology Sales Experiment. MTV. Web: http://www.mtv.com/news/1488027/billboard-sours-on-princes-musicology-sales-experiment/

Duggan, W. (2018, February 28). Apple Music Is Now Worth $10 Billion. U.S News & World Report. Web: https://money.usnews.com/investing/stock-market-news/articles/2018-02-28/apple-inc-aapl-stock

Dziawura, C. (2016, November 16). Exclusive Album Releases raise new concerns in Music Industry. Northeast Valley News. Web: https://tinyurl.com/yboryzv3

Farouky, J. (2007, July 18). Why Prince's Free CD Ploy Worked. Time. Web:
http://content.time.com/time/arts/article/0,8599,1644427,00.html

Forde, E. (2013, July 4). Jay-Z's Samsung deal signals a musical future where the rich
get richer. The Guardian. Web:
https://www.theguardian.com/music/musicblog/2013/jul/04/jay-z-samsung-music-
future

Fossbytes Staff. (2017, May 1). What Are Torrents? How Torrent Works? —
BitTorrenting 101. Fossbytes. Web: https://fossbytes.com/how-torrent-works-what-is-
bittorrenting/

Frankel, T. (2017, July 14). Why musicians are so angry at the world's most popular
music streaming service. Washington Post. Web: https://goo.gl/UVUjpJ

Gladwell, M. (2000). The Tipping Point: How Little Things Can Make a Big
Difference. Boston: Little Brown & Company.

Hamilton, J. (2015, August 12). Columbia House Offered Eight CDs for a Penny, but
Its Life Lessons Were Priceless. Slate. Web:
http://www.slate.com/blogs/browbeat/2015/08/12/columbia_house_bankrupt_mail_or
der_cd_club_s_owner_finally_going_out_of.html

Heisler, Y. (2015, June 25). Revealed: How Much Apple is Paying Artists on Apple
Music (it's Less Than You Might Think). Web: https://bgr.com/2015/06/25/apple-
music-royalty-payments-2/

Hu, C. (2015, November 10). How Music Streaming Is Creating A New Type Of
Superfan. Forbes. Web: https://www.forbes.com/sites/cheriehu/2015/11/10/how-
music-streaming-is-creating-a-new-type-of-superfan/#701d9ed931d6

Hu, C. (2018, January 4). Is Now Really The Best Time To Invest In Music
Royalties? Forbes. Web: https://www.forbes.com/sites/cheriehu/2018/01/04/is-now-
really-the-best-time-to-invest-in-music-royalties/#1be9922b3c8e

Karp, H. (2016, September 8). Music Industry Hits Pause on Exclusive Album-
Release Deals. Wall Street Journal. Web: https://tinyurl.com/yady62mt

Kusek, D. (2005). The Future of Music: Manifesto for a Digital Music Revolution 10:
6-7, 31. Boston: Berklee Press.

La Vecchia, T. (2015, October 12). Bid Farewell: Why Millennials Are Abandoning
Nightclubs. Insider Magazine. Web: https://newtheory.com/bid-farewell-why-
millennials-are-abandoning-the-nightclub-nightlife/

Levin, S. (2018, August 9). Evictions and 'criminalized spaces': the legacy of
Oakland's Ghost Ship fire. The Guardian. Web: https://www.theguardian.com/us-
news/2018/aug/09/oakland-ghost-ship-fire-sentencing-evictions-deaths

Macdougall, K. (2018, March 1). Oakland's Ghost Ship Fire: How Cities Have Responded to Art Spaces One Year Later. MXDWN. Web: https://music.mxdwn.com/2018/03/01/features/oaklands-ghost-ship-fire-how-cities-have-responded-to-art-spaces-one-year-later/

Money, S. (2015, November 24). Fractional-Reserve Banking is Pure Fraud, Part I. Web: http://www.zerohedge.com/news/2015-11-23/fractional-reserve-banking-pure-fraud-part-i

Nevola, J. (2017, November 14). Internet Piracy: The Effects of Streaming Services and the Digital Marketplace. Columbia Science and Technology Law Review. Web: https://tinyurl.com/y72bm7dl

Nielson Staff. (2018). Music Sales Measurement. Nielson. Web: http://www.nielsen.com/us/en/solutions/measurement/music-sales-measurement.html

Parker, C. (2015, September 16). Streaming's Poised to Save the Music Business. Now Apple's Ready to Take Over. Phoenix New Times. Web: https://goo.gl/m91kfK

Plummer, R. (2017, February 12). The clock is ticking for Spotify. BBC News. Web: https://www.bbc.com/news/business-38930699

Press Release. (2007, April 9). 100 Million iPods Sold. Apple. Web: https://goo.gl/XTy5np

Reuters. (2017, September 28). Spotify Is Likely to IPO at a $20 Billion Valuation. Fortune. Web: http://fortune.com/2017/09/28/spotify-ipo-valuation/

Roberts, R. (2016, August 30). What makes for a No. 1 album in the on-demand age of streaming? LA Times. Web: http://www.latimes.com/entertainment/music/la-et-ms-music-charts-20160822-snap-story.html

Robertson, M. (2011, April 18). 25 Jawdropping YouTube Video Facts, Figures & Statistics. TubularInsights. Web: http://tubularinsights.com/youtube-statistics

Rosenthal, R., Flacks, R. (2016). Playing for Change: Music and Musicians in the Service of Social Movements. New York: Routledge.

Sanchez, D. (2018, January 16). What Streaming Music Services Pay (Updated for 2018). Digital Music News. Web: https://www.digitalmusicnews.com/2018/01/16/streaming-music-services-pay-2018/

Schleifer, T., Kafka, P. (2018, January 3). How Spotify solved a $1 billion debt problem that will help it IPO. Recode. Web: https://www.recode.net/2018/1/3/16847786/spotify-tpg-tencent-debt-dragoneer-ipo-music-streaming

Sherwin, A. (2014, September 19). Free U2 album: How the most generous giveaway in music history turned PR disaster. Independent. Web: https://www.independent.co.uk/arts-entertainment/music/features/free-u2-album-how-the-most-generous-giveaway-in-music-history-turned-into-a-pr-disaster-9745028.html

Singleton, M. (2015, May 19). This was Sony Music's contract with Spotify. The Verge. Web: https://www.theverge.com/2015/5/19/8621581/sony-music-spotify-contract

Sisario, B. (2014, November 11). Chief Defends Spotify After Snub by Taylor Swift. New York Times. Web: https://www.nytimes.com/2014/11/12/business/media/taylor-swifts-stand-on-royalties-draws-a-rebuttal-from-spotify.html

Sisario, B. (2016, February 1). Rihanna's 'Anti' Sells Fewer Than 1,000 Copies in U.S., but Some Call It a Hit. New York Times. Web: https://www.nytimes.com/2016/02/02/arts/music/rihanna-anti-chart-tidal-debut-sales.html?ref=topics

Sisario, B. (2017, January 23). TIDAL, Jay Z's Streaming Service, Sells a Stake to Sprint. New York Times. Web: https://www.nytimes.com/2017/01/23/business/media/tidal-streaming-music-jayz-sprint.html?_r=0

Snider, M. (2016, March 31). Jay Z sues previous owners of music service TIDAL. USA Today. Web: https://www.usatoday.com/story/tech/news/2016/03/31/jay-z-sues-previous-owners-music-service-tidal/82460988/

Sohn, G., Fazlullah, A. (2018, February 21). Ajit Pai's Plan Will Take Broadband Away from Poor People. Wired. Web: https://www.wired.com/story/ajit-pais-plan-will-take-broadband-away-from-poor-people/

Solsman, J. (2016, April 12). Study: Streaming Isn't Killing the Music Business — YouTube Is. The Wrap. Web: http://www.thewrap.com/study-streaming-isnt-killing-the-music-business-youtube-is/

Staff Writer. (2003, September 9). 12-Year-Old Sued for Music Downloading. Fox News. Web: https://goo.gl/3nEDiH

Staff. (2018, June 10). About Beatport. Beatport, LLC. Web: http://about.beatport.com/

Staff. (2018, June 10). Traxsource is the modern home for real house music. Web: https://news.traxsource.com/about

Vance, A. (2010, November 6). Chasing Pirates: Inside Microsoft's War Room. New York Times. Web: http://www.nytimes.com/010/11/07/technology/07piracy.html

Variety Staff. (2018, April 3, 2018). Spotify: At Day's Close, What Are the Major Labels' Shares Worth? A Lot. Variety. Web: https://variety.com/2018/biz/news/spotify-at-days-close-what-are-sony-warner-and-universals-shares-worth-a-lot-1202743146/

Waddell, R. (2015, August 4). U2 Closes N. American Leg of Innocence + Experience With 150,000 New York Fans. Billboard. Web: https://www.billboard.com/articles/business/6655667/u2-bruce-springsteen-north-american-innocence-experience-76-million

Walters, N. (2018, January 14). What Is Spotify's Valuation Right Now? The Motley Fool. Web: https://www.fool.com/investing/2018/01/14/what-is-spotifys-valuation-right-now.aspx

Watling, T. (2017, June 30). From sales to streaming. Palatinate. Web: https://goo.gl/LNhtEi

Weise, K. (2012, April 25). Why Half the World Doesn't Have Bank Accounts. Bloomberg Technology. Web: https://www.bloomberg.com/news/articles/2012-04-25/why-half-the-world-doesnt-have-bank-accounts

Whitwam, R. (2017, May 18). Bitcoin Is Bigger Than Ever, And Here's Why That Matters. Forbes. Web: https://www.forbes.com/sites/ryanwhitwam/2017/05/28/bitcoin-is-bigger-than-ever-and-heres-why-that-matters/#f77fc883951f

Williams, R. (2017, February 24). Musician Steve Lacy releases EP recorded entirely on an iPhone. iNews. Web: https://goo.gl/JnEKHo